Divorce & Remarriage

A Redemptive Theology

RUBEL SHELLY

LEAFWOOD

PUBLISHERS

Abilene, TX

Divorce and Remarriage
A Redemptive Theology

Copyright 2007 by Rubel Shelly

ISBN 978-0-89112-519-8

Printed in the United States of America

Cover design by Rick Gibson

For information contact:
Leafwood Publishers, Abilene, Texas
1-877-816-4455 toll free
www.leafwoodpublishers.com

07 08 09 10 11 12 / 7 6 5 4 3 2 1

CONTENTS

Acknowledgements

Leonard Allen has persistently encouraged me to write this book, and I appreciate his friendly motivation at every step along the way. Otherwise, it almost surely would not have been finished. He has given helpful guidance and feedback in the process.

Greg Taylor is both a personal friend and exceptional editor. He read and critiqued the manuscript in its first draft and made very helpful suggestions for improving it.

John York has wrestled with these issues in a local church setting where we partnered in preaching for five years. He also read the first draft and offered beneficial insights.

Emily Polet came to my rescue to proofread the second draft of the book.

I must also acknowledge the many, many people who have heard me make oral presentations on this subject, listened to tapes and CDs, or met with me privately about their situations. Trying to save a troubled marriage, carrying heavy loads of guilt, struggling to understand Scripture, weeping over infidelity, reeling from mistreatment, divorced and abandoned by a former mate, judged by church leaders—people from so many backgrounds have asked me for prayer and guidance. More of them than I can count have asked that I put the interpretations and counsel shared with them into printed form. This book is for them and others who will travel similar paths. I want it to be a source of good information, faithful biblical interpretation, and responsible application of the Word of God to real life.

Finally, my wife was patient with my distraction during intense periods of writing, helped me turn out a manuscript that is more readable than it would have been otherwise, and helps me deal with hurting souls in the course of our shared ministry. It is to *Myra* that this volume is dedicated—with special gratitude for her nurturing heart that has allowed us to remain outside the case studies that appear in this book.

Introduction

This is not a book I ever wanted to write.

Divorce is not a good thing. It disrupts the lives of people who got married with the full and serious intention of living together until death separated them. (Granted, there are probably lots of people who get married these days with intentions far less serious. But few of those people will ever care to read a book such as this one.) Worse still, it disrupts the lives of children born to those people. (I have officiated a number of weddings where the most tension-filled part of the preparation was worry over the participation, seating, and possible interactions of long-divorced, still-bitter parents of bride and/or groom.) And this doesn't begin to take into account the pain and chaos brought into the lives of the extended family of the people involved.

Jared and Megan had been married for less than three weeks, and Megan began acting strangely. She was quiet and withdrawn. Something was going on. And Jared was determined to find out what he could do for his young wife. He loved her devotedly.

For the first few days, he simply tried to be especially attentive and gentle. But nothing changed for the better. Megan, in Jared's words, seemed "distracted" and often seemed to have a "faraway look in her eyes." He thought about asking Megan's mother to intervene. He immediately thought better of it. "We are married now," he said to himself, "and we have to learn to deal with our challenges and problems ourselves."

He set a time to talk with her. He prayed and fasted for a full day before doing so, for he was a devout and sincere man. And he believed that her faith was every bit as genuine as his own. One of the things that had drawn him to her was her sincere piety. Their courtship had reflected the spiritual commitments both of them embraced. There had been no sexual experimentation during their courtship. Jared had counted himself to be among a fortunate minority of men to come to his own wedding a virgin and to have a chaste woman with whom to begin a life of devotion.

"I need to talk with you, Megan," he began. "I want you to be happy. I am doing my best to learn how to be a loving husband to you. But I am worried. You seem so distant. Or maybe that's not the right word. Perhaps I should say 'distracted' or 'preoccupied.' Whatever the correct term, I need you to trust me enough to talk to me about what is going on. If it's something I've done—or failed to do—all you have to do is name it. I promise ..."

"It's not you, Jared," she interrupted. "I'm pregnant. The doctor says I'm three and a half months along. And you can do the math, can't you? This isn't your baby."

She said more, but Jared didn't really hear any of it. He was more astonished than angry. Yet he was angry. He had been wrong about this woman. He had been deceived by her, betrayed by her, played for a fool by her. He would see a lawyer the very next day and start the divorce proceedings, but he knew his life would never be the same. And his mother had doted on Megan.

He didn't know how to clean up such a mess. He just knew he couldn't make a life with Megan. He would be civil and respectful in all the legal papers. "Irreconcilable differences" would be all the courts or he would ever specify for the divorce. He had no desire to destroy Megan, just to be done with this—as quickly and quietly as possible.

There was no way for this to be "painless" for anybody involved. He prayed for hours that night for God to show him a way to get through this unexpected, uninvited ordeal.

Suppose Jared came to you for advice? What would you suggest he do about his dilemma? What would this information do to your opinion of Megan?

The studies done by sociologists, psychologists, and others who research the impact of divorce confirm that divorce is not a good thing. People who divorce once tend to divorce again. The children of people who divorce each other are statistically more likely to get divorced as adults. The children who suffer through the divorce of their parents not only are more likely to divorce someday as adults but are also more likely to do poorly in school, have run-ins with the law, and otherwise struggle to become well-adjusted adults.

So let me say it again—with emphasis. *Divorce is not a good thing!* Anyone who picks up this book looking to find a justification for bailing out of a marriage in trouble should put it down right now. Instead of reading a book about divorce and remarriage, she should go to someone who can help her sort out ways and means for trying to save the relationship. Go to a godly minister of the gospel of Jesus for help. Seek out an experienced Christian counselor. Talk with a mature couple you know whose marriage has lasted for at least 20 years in the face of some real problems—the death of a child, serious illness, or jail time by a family member. Someone in your network of friends and acquaintances can help you get perspective on what you are going through. Somebody can help you exhaust a long list of possibilities you need to explore before you throw in the towel and file for a divorce.

You cannot imagine today the problems you will create for all your tomorrows by getting divorced. You will be alienated not only from a former spouse but from a host of people more closely linked to your mate than to you. The financial repercussions will be horrible. And there will be agonizing times of guilt, compounded by a sense of self-doubt. Even if you are the aggrieved party, you will ask yourself a thousand times if you "drove him to it" or should have seen and reacted to the brewing storm that broke over your marriage.

Ellen lived in a small town. There were no mental health cooperatives. There certainly weren't any Christian counseling centers. If there had been anything of the sort, she would have gone in a heartbeat. She did talk to her physician. And he seemed to be appropriately and genuinely concerned. He offered to prescribe an anti-depressant medication. Beyond that, he encouraged her to "get some help."Her husband had been the "sweetest man I ever met" during their courtship. There had been some sexual activity in the final few months of their engagement, but they ended it about a month before their wedding day. They were both Christians, and they had felt terrible about their sexual liberties—the first sexual experience for either of them.

But they hadn't been married three months before he hit her for the first time. It was only the beginning of more beatings than she could count. That was nine years and two children ago! He was always tearful and apologetic afterwards. There were always flowers and gifts. But there were always more blows to come.

He hit their seven-year-old daughter hard enough last week that he ruptured her left eardrum. Ellen was at her parents' home when she called the preacher for their little church. He encouraged her to come home, give her husband another chance, and "pray real hard for things to work out" for them. He said he was sorry to hear "Ellen's account" of what had been going on. "But I've learned there are always two sides to these things," he said. "You need to go back home and work things out. Even if what you are telling me is true, you don't have scriptural justification for a divorce. You're making yourself look bad by leaving town and going to your parents. Are you sure you aren't involved with anybody, Ellen? Are you just looking for a way out of your marriage?"

Ellen had always been taught that divorce is sinful, unless your mate has been sexually unfaithful to you. She didn't believe for a minute that her abusive husband had committed adultery or that he ever would. He just had this horrible temper. "He may be 'hard as nails,' Ellen," her preacher's words echoed in her head, "but you've got no right to divorce him unless you know for a fact that he has been unfaithful to you."

What would you have advised Ellen, if she had called you instead of the preacher that day?

Divorce is not a good thing. But is it worse than spousal abuse? It seldom answers questions or fixes things. For Ellen, though, a divorce might have protected her and her two children from additional physical abuse. It would not have "saved her good name" in the little town where she had lived. It would not have explained her actions to the church people she loved. And it certainly would not have provided financial security for her and her children.

Ellen made three reconciliation attempts with her husband. In the meanwhile, he had maneuvered himself into the confidence of the minister Ellen had called in her first cry for help. The abusive husband convinced him that, although he had "a bit of a temper," he had never hit Ellen. He had certainly not hit their daughter. And Ellen was prone to be a "drama queen" in describing things anyway.

By the time Ellen was divorced two years later, it was her husband who had made the initial court filing. He accused Ellen of being an unfit mother—and cited her use of anti-depressant medication as part of his proof. He has primary custody of the children now, and Ellen sees them every other weekend. By the way, the church where Ellen and her husband had been members since their marriage disfellowshipped her for being the cause of her family's breakup. She is being treated for severe clinical depression. In a recent letter to Ellen, her former husband told her he hoped she would "find somebody and get married soon" so he could get on with his life and marry the woman he had been dating for the past couple of months.

For the little church that had already excised Ellen's name from its church directory, her decision to marry again would be adultery. She would become the "guilty party" to the former marriage. And her husband would be declared the corresponding "innocent party"—with the right to remarry with the blessing of the church.

Divorce is not a good thing. But when a theological system creates situations where Ellens are first physically abused by their mates and then manipulated, set up, and psychically-spiritually abused, something is definitely not good at still another level. And Ellen's church is now part of the abuse she is suffering. It is pouring salt into the open wound of her broken heart. For all the harm done in the world by people failing to keep their vows of marriage and running to the divorce courts without exhausting all the options for saving their families, there is also incredible harm being done to people by both Catholic and Protestant interpretations of Scripture that turn divorce into something that looks more like gamesmanship than spiritual insight or godly nurture for the battered and broken.

For example, many Protestants have long had a field day with the Roman Catholic option for dealing with failed marriages. Under a system that presumably allows no divorce, a person with enough money and connections can get his or her marriage annulled. So a person married for 37 years and who has two grown and married children—perhaps even a grandchild or two—can be declared never to have been married at all! With the proscription against divorce circumvented, he may then be married by a priest and receive the Eucharist from which he and his bride would otherwise have been excluded. And the person with whom the first "real" marriage is covenanted may be the sixth or eighth person with whom he is known to have had an affair while married to the person who is the mother of his children! What is wrong with this picture?

If Protestant practices were as generally known, Catholics could have an equal sense of outrage at how we handle divorce and remarriage. Churches that permit divorce (with the right of remarriage) only to those who have divorced a mate who has broken the bond of sexual exclusivity by an act of adultery sometimes create absurdities every bit as bizarre as those involving Roman Catholic annulments. Thus a woman is belittled and bullied by a man for years. He is stingy not only with money but even more with affection and affirmation. He forces her to participate in offensive and painful sexual behaviors, all the while telling her how inadequate she is. He tells her repeatedly that she is nothing but a whore to him and that he must have married her in a period of temporary insanity. But if she were ever to meet someone who treated her with kindness and have even one sexual tryst with him, she could be divorced with no right ever to remarry. And the cruel man who put her in that situation could be declared an "innocent party" who could marry again, serve in the church's ministries, and—in most cases—be ordained! What is wrong with this picture?

David came into the preacher's office, almost literally dragging his wife with him. The couple had attended his church several times but were not members. He knew the man's parents from a decade or more ago. They were sincere Christians with little formal education, but they had been pillars in their church. David and his brother had been given advantages their parents had never known.

"Tell him what you've done!" David began, not even seated yet. "You tell him right now!"

The first order of business was for the preacher to get the angry, badgering man to calm down. He talked to David and his wife in the most general of terms to affirm his desire to help them. He wanted them to know that the whole church would try to befriend and assist. "But let's try to talk about this calmly," he pleaded. Speaking first to the sobbing wife and then to the red-faced husband, he asked permission to pray for God's Spirit to fill the place and guide the conversation.

"Now you tell him what you've done!" said David, as soon as an amen was said to the brief prayer. "Tell him that you committed adultery. Tell him that you have slept with that man three times!"

"Yes!" she sobbed. "Yes! I did! But you made me do it, David."

The preacher assumed he was in for a story of how a young husband's neglect had driven his wife into someone else's arms. Hardly! David had brought a friend into their apartment, ordered his wife to undress, and gave the man permission to have sex with her. He sat in a chair beside the bed and watched. He had repeated the scenario with the same man three times over a two-week period.

She told of the three events, and David confirmed them. When asked why he would do such a thing, he explained that he knew within six months of their wedding that he had made a mistake. Since the only way he would ever be free to divorce his wife and remarry was if his wife were to be (unquestionably!) guilty of adultery, he saw to it himself that the deed was done—three times in his immediate presence.

Put your reaction to this scenario into words before reading further. Did the woman's sex with a third party make her an adulteress? Did it set David free to remarry?

Divorce is not a good thing. But might it not be justified as an escape from someone who is mentally ill? Whether it is a divorce that takes place in a marriage that might have been saved with appropriate resources early on or one that is manipulated for the sake of appearances and status or one that happens because one of the partners is seriously mentally ill, there simply isn't a "good" one. So I understand why the God of Israel would say, "I hate divorce!" So do I. And so do most of the people I know who have gone through one. But simply saying that divorce is not a good thing is simplistic and does not take harsh and painful realities into account.

Saying that divorce is not a good thing is not to say that some good people haven't been divorced. It isn't even to say that there are no circumstances under which one is justified in getting divorced. Neither does it mean that somebody who gets a divorce for less-than-noble reasons is to be penalized for the rest of her life for quitting too soon or for having an affair. With the God who has revealed himself in Jesus of Nazareth, repentance leads to real pardon and the opportunity to move on with one's life. Sometimes the emotional and spiritual mess is akin to scrambled eggs— eggs that can't be *un*-scrambled now. But there can be forgiveness and insight from past mistakes, and there can be normalcy in a new life. One can still marry and have a family. God deals with people redemptively. God's people need to do the same.

People who respect Scripture must be convinced we have biblical warrant for what we do. Is there biblical precedent for divorced persons being permitted to move ahead with their lives after serious marital failure? Is there any way to speak with the authority of God in telling a divorcee that he can marry again after a divorce when he was the one who had an affair? Is it right for a church to accept someone into membership who has been divorced and remarried? Or must its leaders investigate the circumstances of that divorce and be convinced that her first marriage ended by no fault of her own? Is it ever acceptable for a person in his second (or later) marriage to be ordained a deacon, pastor, or minister of the gospel?

I have never wanted to write a book whose task is to engage questions this serious and controversial. But I feel both called and compelled to do so for a variety of reasons too complex to give here. My hope in daring to embrace the task is to help some people who have been confused, angered, and alienated by burdens some of us have imposed on them by our mishandling of the Word of God. I would like for this book to be God's instrument for giving guidance and peace to troubled hearts. I pray for God to use it to speak both pardon and hope to some who have felt neither for a long time.

This book has been kept relatively brief and is written in pastoral tones. In the bibliography, there are references to a few scholarly works of history and exegesis on which my conclusions are based. But this book is not an attempt to summarize all that material and explain how it justifies certain positions. It is simpler and more practical. Its goal is to comfort, teach, and guide hurting souls.

This book is also a theological treatment of divorce and remarriage for the sake of church leaders. It is intended to explain that divorce is as "bad" as an adult committing murder and as "innocent" as a youth uttering a swear word when frightened. All are offensive to God, yet all may be pardoned by his grace on the merit of Jesus' death and resurrection. All are sinful and must be abandoned, but nothing is beyond forgiveness when confessed and offered to God. All these actions are indefensible and are never to be taken lightly, yet one who has been guilty of one or more of them must not allow Satan to use the now-pardoned past to rob her of full absolution and the right to live for the future.

A poor method of reading Scripture coupled with a lack of theological reflection has caused some people to believe sincerely that divorce is a sin worse than all others. Thus a person who quit trying in a marriage or one who destroyed a marriage by having an affair has been judged guilty of a sin for which there could be forgiveness but for which there was a lifelong punishment. Repentance could bring forgiveness, but it could not bring the option of a subsequent marriage. I once believed and taught this very thing, but I no longer think such a view represents either the heart or words of God as revealed in Holy Scripture.

Hazel and her just-back-from-World War II husband were trying to make a go of things. Their first child was not quite two when her husband was sent to France. He served honorably, was wounded twice, mustered out just after VJ Day, and had no particular job skills.

He was making good money building houses, but he began to drink a lot. Hazel warned him that she wouldn't put up with that sort of behavior. She was all the more adamant because she was pregnant now. She gave him an ultimatum. Then he staggered home on Friday night just three weeks later. Hazel had meant what she said, so she packed her bags and went to her parents' hometown to start life as a single mother. She never heard from her husband again. Not once.

Hazel started attending church after her baby was born. She learned the gospel, made a commitment to Christ, and was baptized. More than four years after that decision, she met Arthur. He had just moved to the little town in East Tennessee where she was making a living for herself and her children by working as a teacher's aide in the local elementary school.

Hazel and Arthur fell in love. Seven months to the day on which they met, they married. In the second year of their marriage, Hazel got pregnant for a third time. Arthur loved all three of the children in their home and adopted the older two as his own. Hazel's life that had looked so unpromising was happy and fulfilled. Arthur could not have been a more devoted husband or father.

One of the things that bound these two people to each other was their Christian faith and commitment. When their third child was in her first year of elementary school, they faced a crisis. The revival preacher who came through that summer had preached a sermon on Christian marriage. In the process, he lamented how lax people had become toward "the Bible's laws on the sacredness of marriage." And he proceeded to explain that anybody who got a divorce for a reason other than his or her mate's sexual infidelity had sinned. More than that, anyone divorced for a lesser reason who later remarried would be "living in adultery."

Hazel's conscience bothered her so that she could not sleep for nights to come. She finally confided in Arthur that she was afraid she had compromised his spiritual life. For, while she was certain her first husband had probably remarried, she hadn't left him for philandering. She had given him an ultimatum about his drinking. She had left him because of it. If the preacher was right, she had no scriptural grounds for divorce—and thus no right to be married to Arthur.

Hazel and Arthur studied the Bible. Matthew 5:32 and 19:9 seemed to say they were sinning by living together as husband and wife. They got conflicting opinions from more mature Christians whose Bible knowledge and good judgment they trusted. One preacher was particularly convincing—and emphatic. He told them they could go to heaven only if they broke off their "sinful relationship."

Hazel and Arthur got a divorce. Arthur continued to live in the little town and supported Hazel and the three children. When he died at the age of 83, he and Hazel were best friends. Two of their three children are agnostics and say they would never embrace a religion that disrupted their parents' lives and took away their childhood stability. The third child, the oldest of the three, is married to a deacon in the church Hazel and Arthur attended until their deaths.

Is marriage only bed and board? Was the preacher's counsel by which Arthur and Hazel lived for half a century correct? Or was his counsel mistaken and thus responsible for the angry unbelief of two of their three children?

Chapter One lays out the issue of divorce and remarriage from the broader standpoint of its implications for the spiritual lives of thousands upon thousands of people. I outline a general treatment of the subject from certain fundamental principles of the gospel.

Chapters Two and Three review the Old Testament material on the subject of divorce. Because all the Bible's ethical teachings are grounded in the Hebrew Bible, it is important to be clear about what is said there—and, perhaps equally or more importantly, about what is not said there—about this complex subject. Yahweh's own relationship to Israel under the metaphor of marriage and divorce is also traced.

Chapters Four and Five carefully study the words of Jesus. In the context of debate over the teachings of our Old Testament, he spoke with a clear and authoritative voice. Using teaching techniques that are still common, he said things that have been taken with wooden literalism to formulate teachings that are contrary to the fundamental tone of the gospel of God's grace.

Chapters Six and Seven trace the subject of divorce and remarriage in the writings of Paul. The ancient world faced the same problems we lament: widespread marital failure, frequent and easy divorce, and Christian uncertainty over the status of divorced and remarried persons in the church. In his typical style, Paul did not shy away from those hard questions. He gave answers that still serve us well.

Chapter Eight seeks to answer some of the questions that typically surface in response to the presentation of this material. I have tried to include a variety of topics that tend to surface whenever I have spoken on this topic.

The book closes with two brief appendices. The first is "A Letter to Divorced Persons" that seeks to affirm and encourage people who have felt guilty, alienated, and unsupported. The second is "A Letter to Church Leaders" that dares to make some suggestions as to how the church can do a better job of helping people who have been traumatized by the breakup of their marriages.

All the case studies cited in this preface and in later chapters of this book are in place to stimulate reflective thought. If some of them seem almost unbelievable, you should know that most of them come from my own experiences across my years of ministry in various churches. Names, places, and details that could lead to their identification have been changed. The case studies are not included to obfuscate or to confuse. They are told to illustrate how challenging it is to relate the biblical information to the complex life situations of people in a sinful world.

I write this book with the full awareness that there will be people ready to disagree with and challenge its contents. I am not threatened by that, for I do not suppose for a moment that I have the last word on so important and challenging a subject. And I am eager to learn from anyone who sees what I have missed or who corrects my mistakes. This book represents the best I can do with the subject for now. I hope the discussion it stimulates will clarify issues that are still out of focus.

Sometimes our penchant to be right and certain in our doctrine has led us to boil down the complex matrix of Scripture to a series of bullet points, propositions for debate, and systems of thought that grind up people. While trying to be correct, we have sometimes been unmerciful. In our sincere efforts to follow the *words* of God, we may have abandoned the *heart* of God for his people. God is not a computer, and the Bible is not a collection of formulas by which we will be judged—or by which we are permitted to judge one another. God is the Loving Father of all who come to him through Jesus, and the Bible is an invitation for all of us—including the most broken and ashamed—to know him. It is an offer of undeserved pardon. It is the announcement of a fresh start for our lives. Having died to the past, we have been reborn and can start over in the power of the Holy Spirit.

Finally, I write this book with gratitude to God that I have never walked the disorienting path so many others have traveled through a painful divorce. My wonderful wife and I have been married for more than four decades, cherish the relationship we have with our three grown children, and revel now in the delights of nine grandchildren. We harbor no illusion that we are smarter, more mature, or more spiritual than the thousands of others in our peer group whose marriages did not survive. But we are not content to say we were "just lucky." God has blessed us to grow in love for each other over time. (Our friends would say God has had to give her far more grace to deal with my shortcomings than I have needed to live with hers. And they are right!) So this book is not my effort at self-justification after divorce. Neither is it written from a posture of smug superiority toward people whose lives have been different from my own. It is written from the desire to discern and to teach the will of God.

My ultimate hope in all things is that God will be glorified.

Rubel Shelly

CHAPTER ONE

THERE IS (SPIRITUAL) LIFE AFTER DIVORCE

This chapter sets a theological tone for all that follows. It explores the crucial issue of how one should read the Bible. It outlines a high view of Scripture that avoids either lapsing into legalistic readings of the text or veering into subjective grounds for setting it aside. It illustrates a worthier way of handling Scripture from the experience of Jesus and traces its broad implications for the subject of this book.

Christians are right to insist on orthodoxy of doctrine, but we must also learn to insist on (and practice) orthodoxy of community. Perhaps you have heard someone say that it is more important in this Postmodern time to be kind than to be right. From my study of the Gospels, it seems more correct to say that one either misunderstands or is failing to practice what is right if she is not being kind. Mercy is superior to judgment. The gospel is good news for human beings, not hopelessness.

Jesus himself faced this problem of how to handle Scripture within a community of faith. Some of his contemporaries were so adamant that the sabbath should be observed according to correct biblical teaching that they were positively cruel to people. In one setting, for example, a man he healed on a sabbath day was judged harshly for carrying his bedroll home and Jesus was censured for performing the miracle that made him well on a holy day (John 5:1-18). Under normal circumstances, the critics would have been correct on the basis of explicit biblical commandment. The sabbath was not an ordinary day to the children of Abraham, and it was improper to move furniture or otherwise to conduct business as usual on that holy day.

But the rules that govern customary procedure are sometimes inappropriate. Yes, Scripture taught Jesus and his disciples that it was wrong to farm, move furniture, rig pulleys, or do the sort of routine things on Saturday that one could do on the other days of the week. It was "a sabbath to the Lord your God" and Torah explicitly says of its correct observance that "you shall not do any work—you, your son or your daughter, your male or female slave, your livestock, or the alien resident in your towns" (Ex 20:8-11). Every Jewish boy and girl knew the story of the poor soul who dared to violate orthodox doctrine about sabbath observance by picking up wood on that holy day and was sentenced to death for his irreverence (Num 15:32-36). But the rule about behavior under usual and ordinary circumstances was not always appropriate to unusual and extraordinary situations.

As the one who proclaimed himself "Lord even of the sabbath," Jesus articulated a principle of biblical interpretation that we would be wise to keep in mind: "The sabbath was made for humankind, and not humankind for the sabbath" (Mark 2:27-28). In other words, *whenever my reading of some biblical commandment drives me to a doctrinal posture that is oppressive to human beings whom God is trying to redeem, it is time for me to double-check my interpretation of Scripture.* That is precisely the dilemma into which my received understanding of the Bible's teaching on divorce and remarriage put me years ago. Wanting to affirm and uphold the sanctity of marriage, I applied (some!) biblical statements about divorce oppressively. I didn't mean to be barring people from the kingdom of God or making them less likely to pursue Christ, but I did just that. I didn't mean to misrepresent the heart of God for sinful men and women, but I did that too.

Larry married Kaneesha when he was 19 and she was 20. They were students at a Christian college when they met, and a group of friends from the choir they sang in provided their wedding music. It was a beautiful event.

They finished their education, had two children, and divorced when Larry was 28. Kaneesha filed for the divorce on grounds of adultery, and Larry didn't contest the charge. The woman with whom he was having an affair at the time of the divorce was the third since their marriage. Kaneesha had known about the first two, but she had forgiven him and tried her best to make the marriage work. The third betrayal was the final straw.

Larry married the woman with whom he was involved within a month of the divorce. That marriage to Leslie lasted only a bit over two years. Leslie, you see, had less patience with extra-marital affairs than his first wife had shown. So when she found out that Larry was sleeping with a woman he had known long before meeting Leslie, she put him out of their house and out of her life immediately.

The combined effect of two failed marriages was devastating enough to Larry that he sought help from a clinical psychologist. It took very little work on the therapist's part to discover that Larry had been physically and sexually abused as a child. The abuse had created a sexual addict—a term Larry had never heard before the therapist used it of him—who was incapable of establishing healthy interpersonal relationships.

Almost four years later, Larry was visited in the hospital by a friend from his days at the Christian college a decade and a half ago. The friend was preaching for a church across town and had heard of Larry's attempted suicide. He saw him twice before he was discharged from the hospital and frequently over the next two months. He learned that Larry had worked hard toward his healing from the abuse that had set him up to fail in his two doomed-from-the-start marriages.

Larry had met a woman a year ago. Her husband had died of a massive heart attack three years earlier, and she was rearing their daughter alone. Friendship had become dates, and dating had turned into love. Larry tearfully told his friend that he knew he could never marry Evelyn without making her an adulteress. He remembered that from his Bible classes. And he loved Evelyn too much to compromise her and "send her to hell" because of his two divorces. He decided it would just be better to "end it all" and had tried to commit suicide.

His preacher-friend said Larry and Evelyn would be welcome at his church. He told him he didn't believe God was an obstacle to his healing from his past. He said he believed Evelyn might well be God's gift to complete the process of healing.

If Larry was willing, the preacher offered to restudy the issue of divorce and remarriage with him. He confessed that he no longer believed what he, Larry, and their classmates were taught at their Christian college.

One way of reading the Bible is to treat it as a legislative manual. So one goes to it for statutes, commandments, and rules. In the absence of a black-letter law on a subject, the next step is to find a case study that seems to set a precedent for ethics or worship. Finally, in the absence of either a command or working example that is relevant, one searches for rules or precedents that seem related to the subject at hand in order to decide how to proceed. There is some value to this methodical approach to the Bible—as there is value to any systematic study of Scripture. But it has a devastating flaw as well.

The Bible was not written as a law code. Even so, the legal material it contains was never put there to be burdensome. God's purpose with the Ten Commandments, regulations about eating certain foods, or laws about divorce was always to provide loving instruction for his redeemed people. Keeping the commandments would bless his people; defying them would lead them to pain and ruin. So every law encountered in Scripture is to be seen for its loving purpose and not simply affirmed for the duty it imposes. To treat the Bible as little more than a collection of rules does serious injustice to the book, yields endless arguments about what constitutes correct doctrine, and alternately makes people either highly judgmental or terrified of making an interpretive mistake—and being separated from God on account of that mistake.

When his contemporaries tried to drag Jesus into their debate over the relative weight of the hundreds of commandments they had counted in

Torah (i.e., "Which commandment in the law is the greatest?"), he point-ed to the two which embrace all the others. Loving God with one's whole being and loving our neighbors as we love ourselves means not using God's name profanely and leaving the neighbor's property intact. But it means much more. It means learning to read all the commandments through the lens of love. It really isn't enough to refrain from profane uses of the divine name; it is critical to use God's name reverently, adoringly, and worshipfully. It falls short of the divine ideal simply to leave a neigh-bor's snow blower or lawnmower safe in his garage; loving him means helping him fix it when it breaks or using it for his benefit. As Jesus will demonstrate in the Sermon on the Mount, all of God's desires for his human creatures must be read through the lenses of love, grace, and con-cern for the other.

One thing to be said on behalf of people who treat the Bible primarily as a law code is that they seem to be driven to their position by a high view of Scripture. That is, they want no part of playing fast and loose with divine authority. They know that God is God—and they are not. Thus they are unwilling to do anything that smacks of presumption against God. They will not ignore the Bible. They are determined to respect it as the rev-elation of God's heart and mind to humanity. Thus they use such terms as "infallible" and "inerrant" when speaking of the Bible and insist on basing their views of right and wrong in Christian doctrine on the authority of the sacred text.

To say it another way, these "fundamentalist" students of the Bible are on their guard against embracing or giving ground to a "liberal" view that seems capable of setting aside anything in Scripture they dislike or regard as archaic and behind the times. They will have nothing to do with a wave-of-the-hand attitude toward Scripture's affirmation of the bodily resurrec-tion of Christ—or any lesser miracle reported in the text. They will not relax the high moral code of Scripture that protects marriage as the het-erosexual union of one man and one woman who covenant to live togeth-er until death separates them.

What today's liberals and fundamentalists seem not to realize about their "battle for the Bible," however, is that they are *both* highly influenced by cultural factors that make it difficult for them to appreciate the Bible for what it really is. And the single most important issue in our study of divorce and remarriage is to get clear about the nature of Holy Scripture.

Both fundamentalism and liberalism became what they are today because of a cultural turn that you have likely studied under one or more of the following descriptive terms: Renaissance, Enlightenment, Humanism, Modernism, Age of Reason, Scientific Revolution, Rationalism, or some other. These terms point to a cultural shift in eighteenth-century Europe that pushed away the superstition and tyranny of the Dark Ages by means of reason, science, and systematic human inquiry. Rooted in the work of such brilliant souls as Descartes, Hume, and Kant, philosophy and science moved forward with a determined confidence to discover objective truth about all things. Everything would be tested by reason alone, and nothing would be tolerated that could not pass the rigors of modern scientific testing.

Since miracles such as the virgin birth, healing someone who was congenitally blind by mere touch, or being resurrected from the dead are "scientifically impossible," a school of liberal theology arose to reinterpret the Bible free of such "myths." With the scientific method (i.e., repeatability under our observation) as the sole criterion for truth, the Bible itself was no longer "inspired by God" but a human witness to the acts of God—or what superstitious people had presumed to be divine actions—in history. Evolution rather than creation was the true account of human origins, and Jesus was not God in human form but a Jewish prophet with great personal magnetism.

Thus theological liberalism migrated from the German universities to American seminaries to mainline denominational pulpits. Doctrine was no longer meaningful—except for the doctrine of love and brotherhood. Morality was no longer definable—and each person was left to define his or her own values in unique life context. Political influence on behalf of the poor and marginalized became the only real mandate for the liberal church. Enlightenment reason, science, and philosophy redefined the left wing of what was still loosely called Christendom.

The people who rose up to fight what the Age of Reason was doing to religion made the mistake of joining the battle with the presuppositions and methods of Modernism. Thus an army of believers mobilized to defend Scripture as the Word of God to be "taken literally on every point." Creation occurred in seven 24-hour days, and nothing about the theory of evolution had merit. Every racial and gender distinction referenced in Scripture has its contemporary application. All the norms of doctrine, worship, and life portrayed in the New Testament documents must be preserved in the life of the church today. Because of the emphasis of teaching and perpetuating the "fundamentals of the faith," this movement came to be known as Fundamentalism.

This backlash against liberal theology tended to make all issues of biblical interpretation and theology equally urgent. So it was not enough to affirm the deity of Christ and centrality of Scripture but soon became necessary to debate, systematize, and claim infallibility for particular interpretations. Inevitable drawing of lines and severing of fellowship resulted. Each denomination had its distinctive formula for orthodoxy and judged all others by it. In good Enlightenment fashion, each group or individual was sure of finding "absolute truth" by applying the canons of logic to the express statements of the Bible.

Does anyone ever take the time to read Scripture itself? Do the writers of Scripture ever dismiss one another? Does a later writer say that what came before is so dated as to be irrelevant? Do the New Testament evangelists and prophets argue the interpretation of Scripture with Aristotle's logical forms? How did those earliest churches hold together in light of what the text shows to be divergent points of view about worship and lifestyle among its members?

Oscar had failed miserably with regard to his marriage vows. He had neither loved and cherished Karen nor had he "forsaken all others" for her sake. His mother had taught him to love God as a child and had taken him to

Sunday School regularly. But he outgrew all that in his teen years and stopped having anything to do with church.

During his years in college, he lived as he wanted. There was lots of partying. There were more sexual encounters than he could remember. And there was no serious thought of God or spiritual life. Three years after graduation, he married Karen. The marriage didn't have much of a chance, and they both knew it. They were divorced less than two years after they married.

Oscar's "problem" now was that he was smitten by a woman who was different from anybody he had ever known. Yes, Elizabeth was beautiful. But she had an inner charm, dignity, and strength that were even more attractive to him. He dated her a few times and found out quickly that he wasn't getting anywhere with his sexual come-ons. She let him know kindly but unflinchingly that she was a Christian, took her faith seriously, and didn't want to see him again because of his obvious disrespect for women—and for Christian principles.

All that his mother had ever taught him came flooding back to Oscar's mind. Why had he turned his back on Christ? Was that the reason for the mess he was in now—divorced at 28 and rejected by a woman of godly character?

Oscar made up his mind to try to find his way back to Christ. It wasn't to try to connect with Elizabeth, mind you. It was because he wanted what she had for himself. It dawned on him that he was simply tired of being a jerk.

The Bible is not like a detailed set of blueprints for building a house or a roadmap for getting through Manhattan; neither is it a hodgepodge of human writings collected over time. It is the God-breathed revelation of the divine will for human lives. It is not a reference book for people who want to look up spiritual topics to be sure they are right on each one; it is more like a novel in which an unfolding story invites every reader to become a participant as it moves toward the great, climactic scene.

Paul described Scripture this way: "All scripture is inspired by God and is useful for teaching, for reproof, for correction, and for training in righteousness, so that everyone who belongs to God may be proficient, equipped for every good work" (2 Tim 3:16-17). It seems clear from this language that genuine spiritual authority attaches to the Word of God, but we have to be careful when we use that word in today's theological climate. For most of us, the word "authority" suggests a rule. But where is the rule that can cover situations ranging from Larry's to Oscar's to yours?

Suppose we were to think of Scripture more as a compass than a roadmap. That is, it is teaching, reproof, correction, and training in righteousness that keeps us pointed to "true North." From the promises found in the Hebrew Bible through the Four Gospels to the letters to early Christians and churches, everything in the Bible teaches us to move along The Jesus Path. Sometimes there is a law; sometimes an open-ended parable or beguiling riddle; sometimes the fascinating story of a person or family. Some of the material is clearly poetic; some parts are as mundane as a travel diary, genealogy, or declarative sentence; some sections are difficult to classify and would be read one way as poetry and quite differently as straightforward prose.

Scripture is not an end in itself. The end (i.e., goal, target) of the Bible is Jesus. So the words on the page are not merely accounts of God's actions in history but are divine actions themselves. They are "inspired by God" (Gk, *theopneustos*, lit. "God-breathed") and have the same effect attributed to God-breathed words at the very creation of the world. He spoke, and it was done. Light, sky, water, fish, foul—by the very utterance of the words, a reality corresponding to them came into being. Forgiveness, hope, spiritual rebirth, life, new creation—by his utterance of these salvific words over us, a fresh reality corresponding to them comes into being for our lives.

Living under the authority of Scripture is not to be understood as living under the United States Federal Income Tax Code, with its cumbersome attempt to specify every detail of duty and obligation. Oh, there are obligations. But they are the obligations of loving pursuit rather than dutiful compliance. The pursuit of Jesus is oriented by the compass direction of Scripture, but there is no attempt to map out all the possible side-streets and detours one might encounter on the journey. As we pursue and eventually travel The Jesus Path, there are direction-markers to observe. Among them are such moral principles as respecting life and property, keeping promises, submitting to authority, and the like. The difficulty we have staying oriented to these posted markers makes frequent forgiveness necessary, and heaven dispenses it generously.

As Oscar sought to reorient his life to the true-North of The Jesus Path, he knew he needed counsel. So he sought out the pastor of a mainline church. He explained his situation and received counsel.

"Oscar, you seem like a good-hearted soul," began the preacher. "You have called many of your actions 'sins,' but I would prefer to call them 'experimentations' or 'growth-experiences.' We don't sing those old songs about washing away sins by the blood of Jesus here. We have come to understand that God loves all his children unconditionally and only wants us to be happy."

Oscar was a bit confused by what he was hearing. He hadn't been to church in a long time. That much was true. But this counsel didn't just sound foreign to his childhood, it seemed absurd to the sense of guilt he felt for all the pain he had caused.

"Oscar, don't feel guilty about your past," he heard the pastor say. "Press on. Reach for the next adventure. God is on your side."

Living under the authority of Scripture means living in the world of the biblical narrative. Did Adam suffer a horrific penalty for defying God's directive? Did David pay a high price for his marital infidelity? Did Saul of Tarsus later feel terrible guilt for his role in the murder of a Christian evangelist? Yes, so all these stories warn us against disobedience. Yet Adam was not only punished but clothed from his shameful nakedness and given renewed duties for honoring God in a post-Eden world. David suffered a wide variety of terrible consequences from his affair with Bathsheba, but she became his wife and the two of them went on to build a life together that honored the Lord. Saul was pardoned for his hate-crime against Stephen, and we know him better as Paul the evangelist and Apostle to the Gentiles. To live under the authority of Scripture means giving people the grace-option today of living as pardoned people after disobedience, marital failure, or even murder.

The biblical narrative unfolds this story: God created a beautiful, good, and habitable cosmos. Deity created humanity in his own image, and God's intention was to live in open and free community with us. But we chose to rebel against the divine plan and moved deeper into sin and farther away from him. We were disoriented in the cosmos and lost because of our own failures. But the love of God was so great that he undertook a rescue mission and became "God with us" as Jesus of Nazareth. We rejected and killed him! Again, though, God's love for men and women of the human race would not be defeated. So he raised Jesus from the dead by the power of the Holy Spirit. Now the same life-giving, energizing Holy Spirit is at work to transform those who turn back to Jesus, walk the true-North path revealed in Scripture, and gradually learn to embody a new-creation lifestyle.

To live under the authority of this story is less to carry the weight of duties and to feel the sting of failure than it is to believe that the Good News of Christ is true for us. In my personal story of pride that I have never been divorced, the authority of Scripture says that I am nonetheless forgiven of my conceit, taught to see myself as forgiven by grace rather than accepted by good behavior, and sanctioned to share the message that all others may be in relationship with God by grace as well.

Oscar's next visit was with the minister of a church from the same tradition in which his mother had raised him. He remembered the strong affirmations of faith in the Bible he had heard there in his youth. He felt confident the minister would not wave off Scripture as an irrelevance to his situation. He knew he would not dismiss the seriousness of his transgression against Karen.

Indeed, the man listened intently as Oscar related the sorry tale of his personal disobedience and disorientation. It seemed, in fact, that it bothered Oscar more each time he told the story. He wiped away the tears running down his cheeks more than once as he talked.

"Young man," began the preacher, "you have done some terrible things. And I want you to know that I don't blame your wife—uh, Karen, was it?—for divorcing you. In God's sight, she was the 'innocent party' in all your shenanigans."

The words stung Oscar, but he knew they were true. He even felt some degree of strange reassurance in hearing the older man name his behavior for what it really was. He had acted shamelessly and sinfully toward Karen and before God.

"You need to turn your heart back to the Lord in repentance," the minister continued. "He will forgive you of the affairs and adultery. He will wash you clean by the blood of Jesus. And you will need a church home where people will love you, encourage you, and stand by you as you begin to grow in Christ. We will be that church for you, but you need to understand that things would change immediately if you were ever to get married. We would have no choice but to excommunicate you, for you have forever forfeited your right to be married. You would be living in adultery."

The conversation continued for a while, and Oscar thanked the man for his time. He said he would think about everything he had said. It all made sense, and he knew he had no basis to challenge the preacher's statements. It just seemed a bit strange to him that forgiveness of divorce had a "celibate-until-death penalty" that didn't attach to murder or child molestation. Remarriage was the farthest thing from his mind right now. It was probably a good thing that Elizabeth had walked away from him. He could only ruin her life too, according to what he had just heard.

"I might have had more options for my future, if I had just murdered Karen!" he thought. Then he felt guilty for even letting such an idea flash through his mind.

People don't get married with the intention to fail at something so important. Either by virtue of their families' prior arrangement in certain cultures or on the basis of courtship and selecting one's own mate in ours, a man and a woman get married in anticipation of good and holy events. There will be companionship and partnership in life's dark times. There will be someone with whom to share joy and laughter. Sexual intimacy is a special right within marriage—not only for bringing babies into the world but for taking delight in one another and affirming love in a non-verbal way. If you are so blessed, you will have children and partner with each other in rearing them. Maybe you will even live long enough to enjoy your grandchildren. And you will grow old together, meeting each other's emotional and spiritual needs as companions for a lifetime.

But there will be serious challenges to the romantic ideal most people bring to marriage. Your own sinfulness and even that of your premaritally-perfect partner will rear its ugly head. Selfishness will get in the way. Debt, chronic illness, job transfer, a daughter with a handicap, a son who gets in trouble with the law—such things as these expose the fault lines in a relationship and can drive people away from each other. People who once truly cared about each other can become not simply strangers to one another but enemies. Their relationship breaks down. The formal, legal acknowledgment of that breakdown is called *divorce.*

People sometimes get married when they are simply too immature to make such an adult commitment. Some people are not morally fit to marry and will not keep their covenant promise of exclusive devotion and fidelity. Others are so addicted to alcohol or drugs that they can't function in a personal relationship that depends on trust and intimacy. I have even met a few people who were so spiritually empty that they were mean, abusive, and cruel. Maybe some of them were suffering from undiagnosed mental illnesses. What I know for sure is that their marriages won't and can't work—not without a major intervention of some sort and some very serious changes in their behavior.

Oscar made still a third visit to talk with a preacher. Anyone who knew about these visits might have judged that he was "just trying to find somebody to get him off the hook" of the mess he had made. He knew his own heart, though, and that was not the case. If he had been looking for that, his first visit would have been his last. He really wanted to do what was necessary to get his life—in his own words—"back on the right track."

He selected this church, called this preacher, and made this appointment because he—well, he wasn't really sure why. The building wasn't large, and he had never heard of the minister before. But this little church was on the street he most often used to drive to his office. He'd read dozens of those little one-liners on their sign near the road. So why not?

The last of those marquee quotes he read had said this: "*The perfect church for imperfect people.*"

"*Maybe that's my church!*" Oscar said when he read it. Maybe that line was why he decided to call. He sure felt imperfect, all right. So he arrived on time, met the church's 45-ish looking preacher, and started telling his story one more time. This time he actually broke down and sobbed. He apologized more than once for not being able to control his emotions. The minister nodded, didn't seem to be in a hurry, and listened intently.

"*Oscar, thank you for trusting me with that very personal, very painful story,*" he began. "*You sure didn't sugar-coat anything for me! And I respect you for not trying to shift the blame for your divorce by telling me this or that about Karen. You seem so broken. You sound so grieved. To use the language of the Bible, you give me the impression of someone who has genuinely 'repented' of what you have done.*

"*So now that you have shared the bad news of your broken life, please hear me tell you the Good News that Jesus wants you to have right now. God loves you as a mother pities her own child—the way your mother loved you as a little boy when you were going to Sunday School with her and the way I'm sure she loves you still today. And the price for settling up all your sin debts has already been paid at the cross.*"

The preacher began with John 3:16 and explained the gospel to Oscar. By the time he had finished, Oscar had made a decision. He was giving his life to Christ that very day. He would spend the rest of his life trying to serve and honor him. And he wanted his mother to be there when he would be baptized very soon. He was about to blurt out his decision to the preacher. He opened his mouth to begin, but the man who had been talking wasn't through.

"*Oscar, do you know a lady named Elizabeth Brown?*"

"*Why, yes. But...*"

"*Oscar, it just dawned on me that I know something about you. I hadn't put the pieces together until this very moment,*" the minister said. "*Elizabeth is a member of this church. And she came to me several weeks ago to tell me about a man she had met and dated a few times. She told me it hadn't gone well between them and that she'd broken it off and would never see him again."*

"She said she was praying for that man every day. She knew he was not saved, but she wanted him to know Jesus. And she asked me to pray for him too. His name was Oscar."

Churches haven't always been helpful to people in their need to marry wisely, live together in harmony, and meet the sorts of challenges that can threaten a family. On the one hand, some churches are so *laissez faire* toward families that they don't particularly affirm marriage. They fail to put resources in place for married people and refuse to say as much as they should about the perils of divorce to selfish, hard-hearted people. On the other hand, some mistakenly think they are honoring God and doing something that can save marriages by condemning divorce and forbidding remarriage with such a legalistic fervor that they make spiritual orphans of people whose marriages have failed in spite of all they tried to do to save them.

God hates divorce because he knows the ripples of heartache, life disruption, and spiritual wreckage that follow in its wake. Anybody with an iota of spiritual sensitivity who has gone through one hates divorce too. So no Christian could ever call divorce "good" or "wholesome" or "desirable." It certainly was not part of the ideal will of God for his human creatures. But I am convinced I have seen some situations in which divorce was the least evil of many possible responses to a marriage that had broken down. Sometimes it is only a response so drastic as divorce that can force an alcoholic, philanderer, or abuser to face the reality of his or her sin. At other times, it is necessary to protect children from harm. I even wonder about the presumed moral obligation some people feel to try to persuade people to stay together long after their relationship has become nothing more than a "legal shell" that not only doesn't have any personal commitment left but also drains two people of all their spiritual vitality.

I don't have all the answers to the complex questions that can be generated about divorce and remarriage. This book does not propose to answer all your questions about it. But it just might offer you a healthier way to read Scripture—one that will allow you to understand and respond to your questions in a Christ-honoring, redemptive way.

Oscar was baptized on a Sunday morning. It was only a few weeks after his conversation with the preacher about the mess of his life. His mother was there, and she cried tears of joy for her son. Elizabeth was there too.

Oscar participated in Sunday worship, joined a small group at the church, and met with the preacher several more times. One of the things the preacher eventually said to him shocked him. "Oscar, I think you ought to take Elizabeth to dinner sometime," he offered. "Her prayers have been invested in you for a long time now, and I think she would like to see how God is answering them."

To his credit, Oscar was reluctant about asking Elizabeth out for several weeks following that conversation. Nothing about his new life was for the sake of getting her attention. His heart belonged to Christ now! The Spirit of God was doing his gentle transforming work in Oscar, and everybody who knew him saw it happening.

He finally asked her to go to dinner, and she accepted. When Oscar asked the minister what he thought about the possibility of the two of them dating, he smiled and said, "Oscar, I think the two of you may be gifts of God's grace to one another." And they were.

As the dating became serious, the preacher studied the material with them that has become this book. A while later, he officiated at their wedding. Nine years and two children later, they are happy and productive leaders in their church.

One's spiritual life does not have to end when there is a divorce.

The message of the Bible about every human failure focuses on three words—grace, pardon, and healing. I've even wondered aloud several times about ever teaching on "marriage, divorce, and remarriage"—thinking instead that I should teach simply on "ideals, failures, and redemption." Thus I have decided to title this book *Divorce & Remarriage: A Redemptive Theology.*

Divorce is not a sin in its own special class that requires a lifelong penance of remaining single, celibate, and companionless. Can we really bring ourselves to believe that the sinner whose offense is divorce (i.e., covenant-breaking, adultery) has no spiritual option but to live with his failure forever? Can we make ourselves think that the Jesus of Scripture can heal blind eyes, forgive his own murderers, and offer drug traffickers a full range of options for the future but cannot (or will not) heal the broken life of a woman who leaves her husband for a reason other than his sexual infidelity? Worse still, can we really be persuaded that Jesus leaves no option to marry again for someone divorced against her will by a mean-spirited soul who pitched her out?

Jesus did not put this burden on people. Misguided theologians did it. His yoke is easy and his burden is light, but his interpreters have not been as kind.

Jesus' word to anyone who has been guilty of adultery by virtue of divorce is the same that he gave a woman "caught in the very act of committing adultery" whom he rescued from some who were ready to stone her: Go on with your life now. Be grateful that you can. And don't ever do again what has put you in this horrible and unholy situation before God and men.

We cannot turn a blind eye to the harm done by divorce. We must do more to encourage people to pursue options for saving troubled marriages. We dare not pretend that past marital failures don't linger in personal pain and consequences to innocent children. We must teach what the Bible says about repentance for those whose sins have contributed most directly to the failure of a marriage, but we must also teach what the Bible says about faith in the reality of God's forgiveness and healing power. One may choose to live under the authority of Scripture by being grateful for God's grace which provides forgiveness for the past and the chance to begin again.

Chapter Two

The Old Testament on Divorce & Remarriage / Part 1

Although most readers of this book will likely focus on the teachings of Jesus and Paul on divorce, one should remember that their words presume, interpret, and apply the Bible they knew to the subject—our Old Testament. So it is important to deal directly with the Torah and the Prophets before going to the New Testament. Otherwise, we interpret in a vacuum. One of the key elements of Old Testament theology is the motif of Yahweh as rescuer of the weak, oppressed, and enslaved. It sheds new light on the subject of divorce to place it in the context of God's protection of women in Israel.

Christians generally affirm that we accept the sixty-six books of the Holy Bible to be inspired by God and that we look to them for the fundamental and interrelated tasks of instruction, exhortation, and correction for human thought and behavior. Canonical Scripture is the divine repository of revelation in human language and exists to help train believers for both right thinking (i.e., orthodoxy) and right behavior (i.e., orthopraxy). Paul said as much to his young protégé, Timothy (2 Tim 3:16-17). Such texts as this and 2 Peter 1:20-21 are often cited by Christians as summary statements of our attitude toward the Bible.

The problem with this statement is twofold: (1) we are at times less than clear about how inspired Scripture functions as our authoritative guide for spiritual life, and (2) we have a notoriously difficult time in figuring out how the two major sections of canonical Scripture that we call "Old Testament" and "New Testament" relate to each other. (In their statements, of course, both Paul and Peter understood Scripture to refer only to the former.) Both these issues are important enough to justify an extensive exploration beyond the scope of this book.

The answer I believe to be correct on the first of these issues was sketched in Chapter One. Scripture is authoritative to Christian belief and behavior by virtue of its unfolding narrative. It is not merely a book of laws and rules—although several laws (e.g., the Decalogue) are explicitly stated and bound on God's covenant people. Behind the laws are principles we are expected to discern and embrace for the sake of our spiritual lives. In the implicit hierarchy of values reflected in the Bible, principles are higher than laws and give justification for them. For example, there is an Old Testament law that requires people gathering crops to leave the edges of their fields for the poor to reap. Thus, a person whose crops failed or who otherwise had no means of support could both preserve dignity and provide for himself by harvesting grain or produce. Is this rule binding today? May a stingy and hard-hearted entrepreneur in a bustling city claim exemption from duty to the poor because he is not a farmer? Or is the law about fields and harvesting a cultural application of the principle of compassion for one's neighbor? And isn't the principle of loving one's neighbor more expansive than the law about reaping a wheat field?

Beyond both a given law and the spiritual principle that justifies it is the heart of the Lawgiver. The ultimate goal of every rule in Scripture is not simply that one should grasp basic ethical principles but that she would come to know the God from whom the moral nature and duties of a human being arise in the first place. This is to use the word "know" in its biblical sense of familiarity, intimacy, and like-mindedness.

Thus I affirm that to live under the authority of Scripture is to accept God's invitation to be an actor in the unfolding drama of human redemption. It is to enter a story line already well along in its development, to find one's place in the current scene, to act that scene in terms of new-creation righteousness, and to help move the story to its Kingdom of God destination.

Christians are not tyrannized subjects of an omnipotent deity who thunders commandments. That is a pagan view of gods as despots to be appeased because of our fear of them. Jesus came to show us the true face of God as a Loving Father to bewildered and wayward children. As a father gives orders to his children, so God has given commands to us. One of the children who says he loves God while disobeying his commandments is exposed as a liar. But infants who need explicit rules for their behavior are expected to grow up—to discern deeper principles underlying specific rules and, ultimately, to learn to exhibit the heart of their Father.

David had a good marriage for several years. He and Laura had been high school sweethearts. They married after their junior year in college. They had daughters who were nine and five and a half when he began the affair with one of Laura's closest friends. To this day, he insists he doesn't understand how it happened. He and Laura spent a lot of time with the woman and her husband. They even took a couple of vacations together to ski in Colorado. The other couple didn't have a good marriage. In fact, the troubles in their marriage were frequent topics for conversation between Beth and Laura.

When Beth talked to Laura about her husband's emotional detachment from their relationship, it was Laura who asked David to be part of a conversation with them. She believed David could provide some insights for Beth's husband. So he tried to help. He really did.

David's attempts at being helpful involved more conversations with Beth. More and more of those talks were between just the two of them. As he listened and tried to understand, he also tried to console. Holding her hand turned into holding her. Holding her became sexual involvement with her. And she soon became more important to him than Laura. He divorced her and married Beth two months later.

Two years after the remarriage, it dawned on David how much he had lost. He loved Beth. But he had broken Laura's heart, hurt and alienated his two daughters, and lost the respect of people who really mattered to him. It was especially hard to think about his friends from the church where he and Laura once taught the Sunday School class for middle-schoolers.

David had messed up. There was no going back to things as they had been several years ago. He had sinned. He was in a marriage that his friends said was adulterous. He was reading the Bible one day and came across the story of David and Bathsheba. "I wish I had lived under the Old Testament," he thought to himself. "My biblical namesake committed the same sin I have committed. But King David managed to find forgiveness and a way to move on with his life. The New Testament even calls him a 'man after God's heart.' Why isn't there a way out of this mess for me?"

David read the story again. He prayed for God to give him answers. He asked himself: Is there really more grace in the Old Testament than the New? Could that possibly be true?

The second question posed above has to do with figuring out the relationship between the Hebrew Bible and the New Covenant. Someone's first-blush response might be to claim equal value and equal weight for each. Any line in any part of either Testament will be counted as final authority on the subject at hand. But does that really work? How do we live by laws written for such a different place and time? Are we required to make three annual trips to Jerusalem to worship at a Temple that no longer exists? Should we buy fields, plant grain, and leave small sections of those fields for the poor? Are we to keep kosher and worship corporately on Saturday? As you likely know, some sincere students of Scripture argue for some of these practices among Christians today.

Because of the nature of Scripture as narrative, we are obliged to take into account the unfolding nature of the story it tells. If we think of a drama in several acts, we are in the later scenes of the story. Or, if we use the metaphor of infants growing to be adults, we must think of ourselves as living in post-infancy times. This is not to say that every believer is personally mature, but it is to claim that the stage of progressive revelation of God's will for the human race has moved beyond what was appropriate for Abraham or Rahab, Deborah or John the Baptist. These figures in the biblical narrative were actors in earlier scenes. What they experienced and the things made known to them are not necessarily going to be repeated in later ones. We may assume they filled their roles, advanced the story line to a certain point, and we are living in a later act.

What has gone before us is certainly not irrelevant to what is happening now. To the contrary, Paul insisted that awareness of the earlier scenes in the drama is critical to playing our own roles. "For whatever was written in former days was written for our instruction, so that by steadfastness and by the encouragement of the scriptures we might have hope" (Rom 15:4). As we read the ancient texts, we are positioned in history to interpret them more holistically than the earlier characters possibly could have. In Jesus of Nazareth, those persons and insights were brought to "fulfillment" for the sake of all who would follow him. And the specific significance of the fulfillment motif for the subject of divorce and remarriage will be traced in later chapters of this book.

In the most general of terms, then, the Old Testament is critical background for understanding the principles behind some of its laws that may or may not transfer directly to later scenes in the drama. And those laws should be studied carefully for what they tell us of the heart of God for the men and women who had to answer to them. This is a critical principle to keep in mind as we look at Old Testament teaching about divorce and remarriage.

Thus it would seem that what I earlier called a "first-blush response" to the relevance of the Hebrew Bible to Christian moral obligations does not survive theological reflection. It does not work to say that any rule, statement, or law found in either Testament has equivalent value to every other rule, statement, or law one may cite. One must take into account the time, place, and circumstances of the textual data. That is the role of the historical-critical method for Bible study. One must also look behind the rule, statement, or law for the principle it embodies and for the heart of God it reveals. This is why it will be necessary to follow this chapter with material from Jesus and Paul. They are not only actors in later scenes against whose interpretations and understandings we measure our own but are also key players who add new information to all that has gone before. That is the role of biblical theology.

It will surprise some readers of Scripture to discover that the Old Testament contains a number of statements about divorce and remarriage that are contradictory, if the Bible is read as a legal manual. For example, if Deuteronomy 24:1-4 is read as black-letter law to establish an inflexible directive about taking back a former mate, Yahweh not only ordered its violation when he told Hosea to take back his former wife who had been unfaithful to him but modeled the same behavior toward the adulterous nation he divorced for its spiritual adulteries. But if these same texts are read as developments within an unfolding divine drama, they are both consistent and instructive as to how we should deal with certain complex situations we encounter with divorced persons.

Since God's nature is unchanging—he is "the same yesterday, today, and forever"—the one thing we cannot do with the materials in the Hebrew Bible is to dismiss them as irrelevant to persons who have the New Testament in our possession and who live in later scenes of the biblical drama. Ways of caring for the poor may change with different social settings. Even elements of worship may change from animal sacrifices to affirmations of Jesus as the final, definitive sacrifice for sin. But the moral and spiritual obligations of God's covenant people must be understood to reflect his perfect and unchanging nature. Interpreters at our point in history must read Scripture in ways that affirm the continuity of his holy character and compassionate love.

Michelle married Donald in a beautiful church wedding. She was a stunning bride, but most eyes were on Don. He was bright, wealthy, and positively charming. Nobody thought he would marry before age 40. He had been something of a playboy, but Michelle had swept him off his feet.

She was anything but a playgirl! And most of Don's friends believed that fact more than any other drew him to her. She was pretty but not self-possessed with her beauty. She was a godly young woman and was not about to sell her soul for the experience of a man with Don's reputation.

He pursued. She resisted. If anything, it only made him more determined to find out what was going on with her. It was her faith. And he was genuinely impressed.

Don gave up some of his weekend partying for church meetings. Then came a men's Bible study breakfast a couple of his buddies at work asked him to attend. The message of redemptive grace for sinners touched him deeply, and Don offered himself to Christ in all good faith.

By the end of that same year, a courtship was in full bloom. Their wedding was on Valentine's Day. Things went well for almost two years. Then the economy got bumpy, and Don's company was hit particularly hard. The big bonus that had come at year's end for the first two years of their marriage didn't come the third year—but twins did.

Life was hard, but the young family persevered. Somehow they managed to keep their two cars and big house. With everyone else struggling, Michelle and Donald were still prospering. Then we learned the reason why.

Don was arrested in a police raid of area drug dealers. When his friend and minister came to see him at the jail, he cried and explained that one of his old buddies had given him a way to make "good money" about the time his company fell on hard times. He needed the money. He had refused to think about the harm those drugs were doing to people's lives. But he had learned his lesson, would never stray again, and only wanted the preacher to help him keep Michelle from kicking him out of the house.

There was prayer, counseling, accountability, and support—on the part of the church. There was deception, lying, deeper involvement with drug traffickers, and more serious criminal activity—on Don's part.

By the time the full story broke, Michelle—who had suspected more than she had dared believe—was devastated. Don was going away for 12 to 15 years. She would be the sole provider for her twins. And she could never trust her husband again. She didn't know the man he had become.

One of the deacons at her church was an attorney, and she went to him for advice about her situation. He admitted to being in an "awkward situation" when telling her of the legal liabilities she faced because of Don's life of the past couple of years—taxes, criminal investigation, etc. A divorce would be her best legal protection. But the spiritual implications had to be faced as well. Michelle just wanted the nightmare to end.

Genesis 2:24

Teaching about marriage, divorce, and remarriage in the Bible always presumes and occasionally cites the ideal for marriage that is reflected in the Genesis account of Adam and Eve in Eden. The ideal man and woman entered the ideal relationship.

> Then the Lord God said, "It is not good that the man should be alone; I will make him a helper as his partner." So out of the ground the Lord God formed every animal of the field and every bird of the air, and brought them to the man to see what he would call them; and whatever the man called each living creature, that was its name. The man gave names to all cattle, and to the birds of the air, and to every animal of the field; but for the man there was not found a helper as his partner. So the Lord God caused a deep sleep to fall upon the man, and he slept; then he took one of his ribs and closed up its place with flesh. And the rib that the Lord God had taken from the man he made into a woman and brought her to the man. Then the man said,
>
> "This at last is bone of my bones
>> and flesh of my flesh;
> this one shall be called Woman,
>> for out of Man this one was taken."
>
> Therefore a man leaves his father and his mother and clings to his wife, and they become one flesh. And the man and his wife were both naked, and were not ashamed. (Gen 2:18-25)

From the opening lines of Scripture, we are expected to understand that the relationship we call marriage is something more than a phenomenon of natural human social evolution. It exists by the purpose and activity of God. Yahweh called the original human pair into a relationship of intimacy, but the text itself does not use the words of later exegetes and expositors. Where, for example, are words such as "permanent," "inviolable," or even "sacred"? In fact, the balance of the book of Genesis reflects nothing we would usually consider legal material about either contracting a marriage or terminating one.

There is also polygamy in the book of Genesis. It is not named only to be condemned or forbidden. There is legislative silence about it, not only in Genesis but through the early and middle periods of Old Testament history. It is never declared sinful or forbidden, although there are occasional hints that it was not part of the ideal will of the Lord. Abraham, for example, took a second wife, Hagar, at the suggestion of his childless first wife, Sarah. When Abraham conceived Ishmael by her, she was not regarded as a concubine or surrogate mother. She was received "as a wife" by Abraham (Gen 16:1-3; cf. esp. 3b). It would appear that Genesis reflects a non-exclusive view of marriage that prevailed in Ancient Near Eastern cultures generally.

Isaac, the son of Abraham by Sarah, had only one wife. Yet Abraham's grandson, Jacob, took two wives (i.e., Leah and Rachel) and—distinguished from his wives by the specific term—two other women as his "concubines" (Gen 29:15ff). Even after the time of Moses, polygamy was practiced among the Israelites by such notable figures as Gideon (Judg 8:30), Elkanah (1 Sam 1:2), and David (2 Sam 5:13). The best-known polygamist in the Old Testament record is, of course, King Solomon. "Among his wives were seven hundred princesses and three hundred concubines; and his wives turned away his heart" (1 Kgs 11:3).

Just as the Old Testament reflects the prevailing cultural attitude of the Ancient Near East toward polygamy, so does it also appear to reflect—at least by its failure to claim either a distinctive practice from other nations or by the lack of a legal prohibition—the period's prevailing view of divorce and remarriage.

Jesus will later point back to Genesis in order to claim that a divine ideal was inherent in the situation of the original pair—monogamy, no possibility for a "romantic triangle," no mention of divorce, one man and one woman with eyes for each other only. But the original Plan-A ideal state appears to have lasted only briefly. The Old Testament materials after Genesis deal with marriage more practically than idealistically, with more attention to legal issues than to romantic ideals.

Exodus 20:14

Although the concern of this book is divorce and remarriage, it is important to pay attention to the seventh commandment of the Decalogue because of its abiding relevance to the subject. "You shall not commit adultery" (Ex 20:14) is the explicit prohibition to the Israelites of a behavior judged both immoral and criminal by practically all cultures of the Ancient Near East.

In Old Testament literature, to commit adultery (Heb, *naaph*; LXX, *moicheuo*) is to sin by breaking faith or violating one's pledge. It is a sin usually tied to marriage in that the broken faith or pledge typically has to do with sexual fidelity, particularly on the part of a woman. Wealthy males in Ancient Near Eastern cultures are known to have had a range of latitude with regard to plural wives and/or concubines—even to consorting with prostitutes—that women did not have.

It should be noted that to commit fornication (Heb, *zanah*; LXX, *porneuo*) is a behavior manifestly different in nature from adultery in Torah. It is not that fornication was not ethically significant or that premarital sex was not disapproved. But it was clearly viewed as a less serious offense against humankind and deity than adultery, for the penalties that could be imposed for the two actions were vastly different in nature and severity.

Under certain circumstances, adultery was punishable by the death penalty.

> If a man is caught lying with the wife of another man, both of them shall die, the man who lay with the woman as well as the woman. So you shall purge the evil from Israel.

> If there is a young woman, a virgin already engaged to be
> married, and a man meets her in the town and lies with her, you
> shall bring both of them to the gate of that town and stone them
> to death, the young woman because she did not cry for help in the
> town and the man because he violated his neighbor's wife. So you
> shall purge the evil from your midst. (Deut 22:22-24)

A married or engaged (i.e., pledged) woman was considered the exclusive possession of her husband. Because of factors involving family bloodlines and inheritance, a premium was placed on keeping the woman free of sexual contact with a third party. For a woman to consent to sexual intercourse with anyone other than her husband was therefore particularly "evil" because it was a breach of faith; for a man to seduce or be seduced by a married woman would be to make himself liable to death for having "violated his neighbor's wife." The sin in either situation was less the sexual behavior than contravention of the covenantal rights due the woman's husband. This leaves open the possibility at least that other non-sexual behaviors such as abuse or neglect could also be regarded as adulterous. This possibility will emerge in connection with a passage to be explored later in examining the Old Testament materials.

By contrast, in the absence of a marital pledge or covenant, sexual activity between a man and woman was not adultery but fornication. It was therefore subject to a very different outcome for the parties involved.

> If a man meets a virgin who is not engaged, and seizes her and
> lies with her, and they are caught in the act, the man who lay with her
> shall give fifty shekels of silver to the young woman's father, and she
> shall become his wife. Because he violated her he shall not be permit-
> ted to divorce her as long as he lives. (Deut 22:28-29; cf. Ex 22:16-17)

It is interesting that these texts not only serve to distinguish adultery and fornication but also raise the issue of divorce. This makes it apparent that divorce was not only known in cultures around the ancient Israelites but was practiced among them in the time of Moses. Thus one could not claim that every Israelite marriage was "until death do us part"—either death by natural causes or death as a result of execution for adultery. If a man was married as the result of premarital sexual contact with a woman (Deut 22:29b) or if a man slandered his wife by accusing her unjustly of premarital sex (Deut 22:13-19), neither of those men could ever terminate their marriages. These are, in fact, the only two specific situations named in which a man could not divorce his wife. The assumption some have made that divorce was generally forbidden under the Law of Moses is therefore mistaken.

The common understanding of the death penalty with regard to cases of adultery among the Jewish people seems to have been based on a very precise understanding of Deuteronomy 22:22. The condition, "If a man is *caught* lying with the wife of another man," was understood to require acceptable eyewitness testimony in order for the death penalty to apply.[1] As to a woman suspected of adultery on the basis of circumstantial evidence rather than eyewitness testimony, she could be exposed and positively identified to the community as an adulteress by means of the curious ordeal involving the "water of bitterness" (Num 5:11-31). In cases where the woman was thereby exposed, the penalty for her offense was not death but divorce from her husband and disgrace within the larger community. Interestingly, there is no prohibition against her remarriage—although any reasonable likelihood of it may have been quite minimal. As will be seen in the next chapter, Hosea seems not to have considered the death penalty in the case of his wife's notoriously shameful conduct as a woman of adultery. And, as we will see in reading the New Testament materials, neither did Joseph contemplate so dire a fate for Mary when he discovered she was pregnant by someone other than him.

Exodus 21:10-11

The first divorce actually referred to in Torah is Abraham's action when Sarah demanded that he "cast out" Hagar, the wife whom Sarah twice denigrates as "this slave woman" (Gen 21:10). Although Abraham was reluctant to do what Sarah had insisted on because of his attachment to Ishmael, it was eventually Yahweh who intervened to tell him to follow through with the deed. "But God said to Abraham, 'Do not be distressed because of the boy and because of your slave woman; whatever Sarah says to you, do as she tells you, for it is through Isaac that offspring shall be named for you'" (Gen 21:12).

It has already been pointed out that there is no reference to divorce legislation in Genesis. The closest thing to a law regarding divorce in Exodus is found in the context of a series of regulations about the treatment of slaves by the Israelites. "If he takes another wife to himself, he shall not diminish the food, clothing, or marital rights of the first wife. And if he does not do these three things for her, she shall go out without debt, without payment of money" (Ex 21:10-11).

> In Exodus 21:10-11 there is the requirement in the divorce of a wife who is a slave that she must be released without any payment. Presumably this means that she did not have to buy her freedom, though it may also mean that the man did not have to pay her the equivalent of a dowry. Any other wife would be released with the repayment of a dowry, but a slave brought no dowry.[2]

Although this text is generally not part of the discussions of divorce and remarriage in the Old Testament, Instone-Brewer argues that it constitutes a bridge of sorts from the cultures around Israel to its own practices as reflected in the Hebrew Bible. He points out that the legal basis of marriage was an agreement (Heb, *berith*) between two parties that included certain requirements and the penalties that would be imposed for failure to fulfill those requirements.

In the various cultures of the Ancient Near East, it was customary for a bride-price and dowry to be paid in connection with a marriage. Language found both in the larger culture and in the Hebrew Bible reflect practices that were common among a variety of ethnic groups. With some variation, the bride-price was typically paid by the groom to the father of his bride in order to seal the betrothal. A dowry was then paid by the bride's father to the bride.

> The dowry could be regarded as the equivalent to the daughter's share of the family estate, held in trust for her by her husband. In effect, therefore, the payment by the bride's father helped the couple to establish their home.
>
> The dowry also gave personal security to the bride. The dowry continued to belong to the bride, so if her husband died or divorced her, she had money to live on. She might also get a portion of the estate in addition to her dowry. The only exception was when the wife caused the divorce. In some arrangements the wife would get only half the dowry in this case, though usually she lost all rights to the dowry.
>
> These payments also added security to the marriage itself. The bride-price, which was paid by the groom to the bride's father, represented many months [sic] wages. This helped to insure that marriage was not entered into lightly. The whole system of payments was weighted against divorce, because whoever caused the divorce was penalized financially.[3]

Scot and Judy had decided they would not have any children. Scot would have preferred it otherwise, but Judy had been adamant from the time their courtship became serious. "I am not going to be a mother," she said. "I intend to use my education to pursue a career path, and I can't see being tied down with kids."

Scot loved her enough that he agreed. There would be no children, and he would have a vasectomy to be sure of it.

Four months after their wedding, Judy missed a period and bought a pregnancy test kit. The vasectomy had failed, and she was pregnant with Scot's child. So she went to her obstetrician, confirmed the pregnancy, and scheduled the procedure for the next morning to abort the baby she was carrying.

She told Scot of the pregnancy and about her plan that night. Judy would need him to take a sick day and take her to the outpatient surgery center at

6:30 the next morning. He did everything he could to talk her out of it. He believed abortion in situations like theirs was unjustified, and he wasn't sure he could live with the decision.

"It's not your decision to make!" Judy shot back. "This is all your fault. We agreed there would be no children. And I have made the decision to stay with that commitment. I am not going to be a mother."

Judy had the abortion. Things were never the same between the two of them again. And the marriage ended within a year.

Shortly after the divorce was final, Scot asked to talk with one of the elders he knew well. He asked for confidentiality about their conversation and told the story about his divorce. "From your understanding of what the Bible teaches, can I remarry someday?" he asked.

What if you were that elder? What would you tell Scot?

Instone-Brewer argues for two conclusions from the Old Testament material that help clarify much of what is found there.

First, Instone-Brewer claims that biblical students have been careless in reading later theological distinctions between "covenant" (i.e., a grace-based relationship) and "contract" (i.e., a law-based agreement) into the biblical material on marriage. The single Hebrew word *berith* covers both concepts, and it is only in the later Hebrew prophets that the emphasis moves away from conditional agreements between Yahweh and his people (i.e., deuteronomic theology) to the clear promise that God would keep his promises even if his people should prove faithless.[4] Thus the clearer term for the marital arrangements envisioned in the Hebrew Bible is likely our English "marriage contract." And, as with most contracts, a principal motivation for honoring it was a financial one.

Second, in addition to whatever additional oral or written stipulations might be involved in a Hebrew marriage contract, there were certain basic rights and expectations that were understood to apply to every marriage. These unwritten stipulations were in some sense more to the essence of a Jewish marriage than the written provisions. For example, there was not likely to be a written contract of marriage except in the case of an unusually large dowry. Such "usual and customary" negative matters as the death penalty for adultery were seldom written into the marital document, although the potential for a death penalty for this crime is found throughout the Ancient Near East. Exodus 21:10-11 appears to state the "usual and customary" positive support that a man was obligated to provide his wife. By stipulating that a man "shall not diminish the food, clothing, or marital rights of the first wife"—even if that first wife had been a slave purchased for him—we are probably reading what that culture took for granted to the degree that it was seldom specified in written documents. "It was generally assumed by rabbinic interpreters that this right extended to free wives as well as slave wives. This was presumably based on the logic that any right that a slave had would certainly also be shared by a free person."[5]

To Instone-Brewer's two conclusions from this text, there is also the possibility of a third reasonable inference. That a man was obliged always to provide food, clothing, and conjugal rights to his mate may well lie behind Yahweh's acquiescence to the dismissal of Hagar from Abraham's home in the Genesis story.

> When Hagar conceived, "her mistress was despised in her eyes" (16:4), which led to Sarah's treating her harshly so that Hagar fled into the desert (16:5-6). Read in the light of Exodus 21:7-11, and given both Sarah's and Hagar's attitudes, it would have been very difficult for Abraham to perform his husbandly responsibilities for both Sarah and Hagar at the same time. Since he could no longer treat Hagar as a wife he would have been obligated by Exodus 21:7-11 (had it been in effect) to let her go free. God's command in Genesis 21 is thus consistent with the later Mosaic law.[6]

To this point in examining the Old Testament texts, we have set the stage for interpreting a statement in Deuteronomy that has been the focal point of Jewish and Christian interpretation. In the next chapter, we will deal with that controversial text in view of the insights now at our disposal from the generally ignored background that we have just explored from earlier sections of Torah.

CHAPTER THREE

THE OLD TESTAMENT ON
DIVORCE & REMARRIAGE / PART 2

This chapter argues that Deuteronomy 24 is a statute intended to demonstrate Yahweh's concern for the cultural disadvan-
tage of women in antiquity. Israelite women put away by their
husbands were to be guaranteed protection from future harass-
ment by them. A divorcee had the right and likelihood of remarriage. Under the metaphor of divorce, Yahweh even explains his
own actions toward a persistently rebellious Israel.

The previous chapter explored elements of Old Testament teaching relevant to divorce and remarriage from Genesis and Exodus. It is important to keep this material in mind as background for the texts to be studied
in this chapter. In fact, I fear it is the general tendency to read and apply
these later texts without such background that creates many of our interpretive problems. Yahweh was concerned to protect seduced (i.e., raped)
women or slaves taken as wives. Everything presumed in those protective
statutes carries over now as background to the provisions made for free
women who were married in Israel. Practices of various cultures surrounding the Israelites allowed men to abuse women generally and their wives in
particular. Israel's "missionary purpose" of being a light to the nations
required that such behaviors be repudiated among the Chosen People.

Against the ill-treatment and exploitation of females that was rooted in male hardness of heart against them, Israel was called to put the heart of Yahweh on display. The "certificate of divorce" was therefore anything but a penalty or punishment. It was a legislative protection for women and was designed to implement the sentiment of psalms such as this one:

> Give justice to the weak and the orphan;
>> maintain the right of the lowly and the destitute.
> Rescue the weak and the needy;
>> deliver them from the hand of the wicked. (Psa 82:3-4)

Deuteronomy 24:1-4

An important Old Testament text that not only builds on what has gone before but also links directly to what Jesus would later say about divorce and remarriage comes from the final book of Torah. It is not a text that condemns divorce; to the contrary, it proves that divorce was permitted among the Israelites. It gave protection to a divorced woman by guaranteeing her the right of remarriage following rejection by her first husband.

> Suppose a man enters into marriage with a woman, but she does not please him because he finds something objectionable about her, and so he writes her a certificate of divorce, puts it in her hand, and sends her out of his house; she then leaves his house and goes off to become another man's wife. Then suppose the second man dislikes her, writes her a bill of divorce, puts it in her hand, and sends her out of his house (or the second man who married her dies); her first husband, who sent her away, is not permitted to take her again to be his wife after she has been defiled; for that would be abhorrent to the Lord, and you shall not bring guilt on the land that the Lord your God is giving you as a possession. (Deut 24:1-4)

This is clearly an instance of case law that is designed to clarify existing practices. Before going further in trying to understand its larger significance, notice a few obvious things about this text. First, it does not create divorce in Israel but acknowledges something that is already a cultural practice among the people. Second, it does not attempt to eliminate an existing cultural practice by forbidding divorce from that point forward. Third, it not only assumes but provides the clear legal authorization for a divorced woman who has "something objectionable about her" to remarry. Fourth, its only explicit prohibition is against the first husband taking the divorced woman back in case she should be divorced by her second husband or if that husband were to die.

Although later rabbinic and Christian debate around this passage would focus attention on the meaning of the phrase "something indecent about her," that debate is clearly a shift away from the original intent of this text. Deuteronomy 24 is not defining the appropriate conditions under which one may divorce and remarry. It is concerned to prohibit the subsequent marriage of the original couple after a divorce and remarriage. In other words, the thrust of this long and complex statement is to forbid the one action that some people have offered as the only acceptable solution for those who got married years ago, then divorced, and moved on to remarry other persons—that they must return to their original marriage partners. In light of this text, those who argue that legally divorced persons are "still married to each other in the eyes of God" are seriously mistaken; people divorced by legal statute are divorced in God's eyes, and what God says is separated let no man claim to be joined together. In light of this text, those who urge remarried persons to divorce their present mates in order to return to a prior spouse are ethically wrong; they are offering divorce as the corrective to divorce, and those whom God has joined together let no one separate.

Gerry grew up in a very legalistic religious environment, got his training for ministry in an unaccredited "school of preaching" of the same stripe, and married Carolyn the same weekend he received his diploma.

Three churches and three children later, Gerry and Carolyn were "stars" in their circle. Gerry frequently spoke at the annual Bible Lectures of his alma mater. He was in demand for summer revivals. He had found a particular niche as a writer for a couple of religious journals whose task was to "defend the faith" against all comers. So it shocked everyone who knew them when Gerry suddenly resigned his preaching position and confessed to "serious moral failure" in his letter of resignation.

Carolyn tried to work things out with Gerry. But she eventually filed for divorce after learning that Gerry's "serious moral failure" had been a series of affairs with women in the churches he had served. There were at least three women in the church from which he had resigned so suddenly who had been involved with him. Gerry's letter of resignation was sparked when one of them went to an elder of the church about their affair.

Carolyn and the three children soon moved to be near her parents and to start life without him. Gerry simply dropped out of sight from his former church, hometown, and family. The next anyone heard from him, he was in the Northwest and was working for a hardware company. His outgoing personality made him a natural candidate for a management position, and he did well in his new career.

Four years later, Carolyn married a widower from the town where she and her three children had settled. The two of them, the one of her children still in high school, and her husband's daughter who was in the same grade at the local school seemed to be doing well. Although neither she nor her children had any direct contact with Gerry, one of the girls learned that her father had left his job with the hardware company, remarried, and returned to the ministry. Given the no-remarriage-for-adulterers position all of them embraced—having been taught it by their father—they were at a loss to make sense of it.

Gerry had indeed found a preaching position with a church from his old circle of acquaintances. He convinced its leaders with this line of reasoning: "When I had some problems several years ago, I confessed them to God and to the church and was forgiven. Carolyn took me back, we lived together as husband and wife, but she just couldn't forgive and forget. When she divorced me, she had no scriptural grounds for it. Although the courts said we were divorced, I know we were still married in the eyes of God. So when she got married again,

I knew I had been set free from my bond to her. I believe I have every right to be married now and to resume God's calling on my life to preach the gospel."

The church's leaders found his argument to be biblically sound and convincing. Gerry is not only preaching for a church again but has started publishing a religious journal.

In its Old Testament context, Deuteronomy 24:1-4 is about the protection of women and the elevation of their status as human beings. It has already been demonstrated that the cultures of the Ancient Near East had a view of females that regarded them more as property than persons. Status, rights, and legal prerogatives belonged almost exclusively with males. There are several Old Testament texts that modern readers hardly notice because of our notions of gender equality that were utterly revolutionary for their time and place in antiquity.[7] None of the affirmations of women or advances made toward their full personhood in society may be quite so significant as this one.

Leaving the issue of defining the unspecified "something objectionable about her" of this text until we come to Jesus' discussion of it in the New Testament, the prohibition of a man taking back a woman he once saw fit to divorce (for whatever reason!) seems clearly to be a case of protecting her from exploitation by an unscrupulous man.

Our best evidence is that the male-dominated cultures around Israel were not reluctant to abuse and exploit women to shameless extremes. Not only were their religions often connected to fertility rites that were often little more than orgies in the name of religion but women could be married, divorced, and later "reclaimed" if they should happen to come into inheritances, build their own economic base, or secure property (including children) by a subsequent husband. For that matter, if a former husband simply wanted to spite a woman by interrupting her efforts to build a new life, he could do so on a whim. Deuteronomy 24 effectively saw to it that females in the community of Israel were afforded a status and dignity that kept them from such degradation and heartlessness.

The law of the divorce certificate marks a very distinctive difference between the Pentateuch and other ancient Near Eastern laws. It provided a clean and proper end to a broken marriage. In other ancient Near Eastern cultures, the man could neglect his wife and then reclaim her within five years, even if she had remarried in the meantime. The Middle Assyrian law #36 states:

> If her husband has gone off to the fields,.... If she has gone to live with a(nother) husband before the five years and has also borne children, her husband upon coming back shall get her back and her children as well because she did not respect the marriage covenant but got married.

The law of Deuteronomy 24 meant that a man could not simply reclaim his wife. He had to give her a certificate that stated that she was free to remarry. At the same time he would presumably have to settle the return of the dowry, so that the wife would have some money to live on....

As originally intended, the Pentateuch gave women greater freedom than any other ancient Near Eastern law. It gave divorced women the documentary evidence of their divorce, which enabled them to remarry without fear of counterclaims some time in the future from their former husbands.[8]

This understanding of Deuteronomy 24 reflects the contractual nature of marriage as it was viewed at that point in time in Hebrew culture. The regulation set forth here likely would have the effect of curbing at least some hasty divorces by requiring a legitimate cause for the divorce action, bringing it before a public official, and the preparation of a legal document (Heb, *get*)—as well as returning all or part of the dowry. Although the divorce action was originally seen as the exclusive right of the husband, the rabbis eventually made provision that a woman could sue for divorce under certain conditions and the court would require her husband to consent to the divorce certificate.[9]

Ezra 9-10

Ezra was a man of priestly background who was a "scribe skilled in the law of Moses" (7:1-4) and who led a second group of Jews back from exile in Babylon in 458 B.C. He was particularly distressed over the spiritual condition of the people in their desolated homeland. So he challenged the people not only to rebuild the Temple at Jerusalem but also to take seriously the Torah their ancestors had neglected through unbelief. His work is summarized in these words: "Ezra had set his heart to study the law of the Lord, and to do it, and to teach the statutes and ordinances in Israel" (7:10).

With his heart set on Torah, one can only imagine Ezra's dismay at finding out that many in Judah—including leaders of the people—had intermarried with "the Canaanites, the Hittites, the Perizzites, the Jebusites, the Ammonites, the Moabites, the Egyptians, and the Amorites" (9:1; cf. Neh 13:23-39). The Law of Moses specifically prohibited such mixed marriages in Deuteronomy 7:1-5 and 23:3-6. Yet the purpose behind the prohibition was clearly not racial but spiritual.[10] Indeed, such non-Jewish women as Ruth (Moabite) and Rahab (Canaanite) not only married Jewish men but also figure positively in the Old Testament story and are in the lineage of Jesus. Even Moses married a Cushite woman—over the protest of Aaron and Miriam but with the blessing of Yahweh (Num 12:1ff). The problem of mixed marriages was not blood lines but Israel's exclusive devotion to the God with whom they covenanted at Sinai. The marriages that distressed Ezra were those formed with women who still worshipped their idol deities and who would—as Solomon's foreign wives had done with him—turn the hearts of their husbands and children away from Yahweh.

So Ezra, the Torah scholar and teacher among the returned exiles, saw a crisis before the nation. The world's superpower of the time was the Persian Empire, and it was aggressively promoting the merging of diverse religious beliefs and systems into a grand syncretistic arrangement. The goal was very similar to that of some today who would prefer to see Christianity abandon its exclusive devotion to Jesus as the one alone who can provide access to God by virtue of his role as the Way, the Truth, and the Life. Ezra called instead for the revival of Yahwism and challenged the people to separate themselves from idolatry and all its trappings. He prayed before the people and lamented to Yahweh: "Shall we break your commandments again and intermarry with the peoples who practice these abominations?" (9:14).

In a revival of fervor for the Lord, the people confessed their faithlessness in this matter and their leaders pledged to put away both their pagan wives and the children they had fathered by them (10:3-5). Over a three-month period, the mixed marriages were systematically dissolved (10:12-44)—with a total of 113 recorded in the text of the book of Ezra. Interestingly, a man named Shecaniah told Ezra to lead the people to "send away all these wives and their children" in an orderly fashion. He was particularly urgent about one matter in particular: "And let it be done according to the law" (10:3). Some scholars raise the question as to whether Shecaniah may have had Deuteronomy 24:1-4 in mind. If so, were the pagan religious practices of a man's foreign wife reckoned as "something objectionable about her" that justified divorcing her?

Malachi 2:10-16

After reading about the divorce proceedings called for by a Torah scholar to protect the spiritual integrity of Israel, it is interesting to note that another prophet in Israel during the period just after the exile in Babylon is the one who spoke these words in Yahweh's name: "I hate divorce." Does Malachi trump Ezra? Or was Ezra justified in his interpretation of Torah?

The most common use of the statement found at Malachi 2:16 is to offer it as a blanket condemnation of divorce. A close reading of the context, however, revises one's opinion. It is actually a judgment against divorces of a particular type and not a statement that God is opposed to any and all divorce. To interpret the statement in the latter way puts one in the situation of always having to look for exceptions and ways to justify such texts as have already been studied in this chapter.

Malachi's ministry took place only slightly prior to those of Ezra and Nehemiah. The text in question seems to be his way of dealing with an element of the same problem that Ezra would later address with his call for the people of Judah to divorce their pagan wives. He rebukes the people who have taken foreign wives; such persons have "married the daughter of a foreign god" (2:11). But he raises a point that is not mentioned in the Ezra material. In order to take their pagan wives, many a man of Judah had committed an even more fundamental offense against a prior companion. Malachi indicts any such person by explaining why the Lord's blessings are being withheld from him: "Because the Lord was a witness between you and the wife of your youth, to whom you have been faithless, though she is your companion and your wife by covenant" (2:14b).

Whereas Ezra would indict the people who were married to and compromised by pagan women, Malachi points to the fact that at least some who had taken foreign wives had first shown a particular callousness toward their Jewish wives by divorcing them. Thus, "what is condemned in context is not necessarily every divorce under every condition—as if the text is opposed to the actions of Ezra and Nehemiah—but specifically the divorce of innocent Jewish wives simply because their husbands prefer foreign wives to their Jewish ones."[11] These Jewish women were not being divorced on the basis of "something objectionable" in their behavior (cf. Deut 24:1) but because of the unconscionable faithlessness of their husbands. So while the consistent tone of the Old Testament is against divorce because it is the breaking of a covenant or marital contract, the harsh language of this text is about a particularly heartless form of divorce without justification of any sort.

Hosea 1-3

Finally, there is the Old Testament case study of Hosea's divorce from Gomer, its explanatory value for Yahweh's relationship to Israel, and certain implications of all this for interpreting the unfolding narrative of Scripture. In my opinion, it is necessary to draw one critical insight above all others from the book of Hosea—the folly of trying to use the Bible as a legal guide to solving the host of problems we face relative to divorce and remarriage.

With his contemporary Amos, Hosea stands at the beginning of the "writing prophets" of Israel. He has the distinction of being the only writing prophet from the Northern Kingdom. He pleaded with his own nation for half a century or more (ca. 760-710 B.C.) to turn back to the Lord. His warnings went unheeded, and Israel—typically referred to in the book by the name of its largest tribe, Ephraim—fell to the Assyrians.

Dottie and Ed married immediately after graduating from college. She was not unattractive, but Dottie was quiet, had dated very little, and was quite insecure. Ed had practically no social skills and had met Dottie in an upper-division math class. There were no bells and whistles to their romance, but they dated no one else for the final two years of college.

Their seventeen-year marriage was stoic. Both of them worked, except for the three months of leave Dottie took when their daughter was born. Ed had wanted a son to carry his family name, and his response to several friends from their church at his daughter's birth had been, "Maybe I'll get my boy next time." There would be no more children.

Ed's mother dominated his life. He, Dottie, and their daughter ate dinner at her house every Monday night. She had never liked Dottie, advised Ed not to marry her, and belittled her mercilessly in front of her granddaughter. Ed didn't play golf on Saturdays. He mowed his mother's yard and spent the morning with her. He only occasionally attended his daughter's dance and music recitals.

Four years before Dottie divorced him, Ed began accusing her of having an affair with her boss. It was not true, but Ed could not be dissuaded from accusing her. He even hired a private detective to—in his words—"get the goods on them." No incriminating evidence was found, and the investigator told Ed that he never saw anything suspicious about their behavior. He actually told him, "I think you're wasting your money, paying me to watch your wife."

The accusations not only continued but escalated. He blurted out an accusation at his mother's home one Monday night over dinner. The matriarch took her son's word at face value, and the 13-year-old daughter fled the family dinner table in tears. Dottie said she would not go back to her mother-in-law's home without an apology, and none was ever made. Two years after the divorce, Dottie found out that Ed had met secretly with their church's elders and accused her of being unfaithful to him. They listened to him. They did not contact Dottie. They did not follow up with Ed.

The rancor in their home became so intense that Dottie gave Ed the ultimatum of marriage counseling or divorce. He said, "You may need counseling, but I'm just fine!" His reaction did not soften over the next eight months, so she filed for divorce. "My daughter and I could never have a minute's peace around him," Dottie said. "I felt like I had to get a divorce or lose my mind."

Ed had a second meeting with the elders of his church after being served with divorce papers. This time they decided they had to do something. So they sent Dottie a certified letter telling her she would be disfellowshipped by the church if she followed through with the divorce.

Hosea's ministry and his message to Israel were set against the background of his tragic family life. Hosea married Gomer, had three children with her, and suffered the humiliation of her repeated adulteries. Finally, he divorced her. "She is not my wife, and I am not her husband," said Hosea to his younger son—language found in certain ancient divorce documents. Time passed. Hosea continued to speak the prophetic word the Lord gave him for Israel. Yet he never stopped caring for his beloved Gomer. He finally took her again as his wife (2:19), and it appears that he did so in obedience to a command from God. "The Lord said to me again, 'Go, love a woman who has a lover and is an adulteress, just as the Lord loves the people of Israel, though they turn to other gods and love raisin cakes' " (3:1). The story is filled with pathos and compassion. A good man is betrayed by his wife, nevertheless exhibits undying love for her, and eventually is reunited with the woman for whose love and companionship he has yearned.

Hosea's experiences with Gomer are skillfully interwoven with those between Yahweh and Israel. The Lord loved Israel and took that nation to be his covenant people and bride. Yet the people were guilty of repeated breaches of faith (i.e., spiritual adultery) with the idol gods of the nations around them. In the book of Hosea, he is on the verge of divorcing Israel for her faithlessness but apparently does not go as far as Hosea did in putting away Gomer. By the time of Jeremiah, however, Yahweh is represented as having divorced Israel under the provision of Deuteronomy 24. "She saw that for all the adulteries of that faithless one, Israel, I had sent her away with a decree of divorce," the Lord told the Southern Kingdom, "yet her false sister Judah did not fear, but she too went and played the whore" (Jer 3:8).

Does the Hosea story not caution us against playing a rule in one biblical text against a different rule in another text about divorce and remarriage? Does it not illustrate that laws are answerable to principles that, in turn, are reflections of God himself? Can we not see here the danger of legalism with the biblical texts?

If we attempt to make Deuteronomy 24:1-4 something other than a requirement for formalizing divorces with documentation that freed people to marry again, Yahweh has ordered Hosea to sin by remarrying the wife whom he had previously divorced. Worse still, it pictures God himself as willing to take back a divorced Israel to be his wife. The laws given at various times about divorce and remarriage were meant as correctives to abuses at hand. Behind each of those laws is the eternal purpose of God to act redemptively on behalf of his sinful human creatures. And we must be careful in every generation to guard against interpreting those laws in ways that cancel the intention behind them.

In summary, then, the key Old Testament texts relating to divorce and remarriage that have been surveyed in two chapters reveal the following important facts:

First, marriage exists by the will and purpose of God, and fidelity within marriage is the divine ideal.

Second, marriage is created when human beings make formal pledges to one another in the form of a *berith*, a Hebrew term variously understood as a "contract" or "covenant" with mutual benefits and mutual responsibilities.

Third, divorce occurred in the larger cultural context of biblical actors and events for a variety of causes and often with harsh and cruel consequences, especially for women and children.

Fourth, statutes were instituted in Israel whose clear purpose was not only to discourage the thoughtless and quick resort to divorce on the part of males but also to protect females from some of the more egregious forms of abuse ancient cultures tolerated for women.

Fifth, in cases where sexual infidelity was particularly flagrant and the parties were shameless in their evil behaviors, the death penalty was a potential consequence for both the man and woman involved.

Sixth, remarriage was customary and expected following divorce under the Mosaic Law. It was specifically authorized for women by the official divorce certificate a man was ordered to give a wife being discharged from his family.

Seventh, divorced and remarried persons were not excluded from the covenant community or denied the right to participate in its religious rites.

In their total experience as Yahweh's Chosen People, the Israelites were challenged to rise above the pagan norms and lifestyles of the people among whom they lived for the sake of bearing his glory before unbelievers. Their failure to honor the Lord in their marriages was certainly displeasing to Yahweh. It resulted in predictable social decay and blighted personal lives. And it exposed situations where God acted to deal with his people mercifully in some instances (i.e., when they exhibited penitent hearts) and punitively in others (i.e., when their conduct was rebellious). While divorce was not part of the divine ideal, it was acknowledged as a reality among the people of Israel and was not presumed to revoke one's standing as a member of the covenant people of God.

CHAPTER FOUR

JESUS ON DIVORCE AND REMARRIAGE
PART 1

For Christians, the final authority for determining the meaning of Holy Scripture is always Jesus. He models, interprets, and applies the Word of God. The Kingdom of God is among us through his presence. This chapter explores two things: (1) Jesus' method of dealing with Scripture generally and (2) his specific comments on divorce in Matthew's Sermon on the Mount.

From the time of his youth, Jesus of Nazareth was devoted to the study of Scripture. At the tender age of 12, he "astonished" adults with his grasp of it (Luke 2:41-47). We presume he continued to explore Torah, the Writings, and the Psalter as he matured (Luke 2:52). After the Spirit came upon him at his baptism by John, he returned to Nazareth, went to the synagogue in his hometown, and was asked to read from the Prophets (Luke 4:16ff). He both taught directly from the Hebrew Bible and fielded questions about its interpretation throughout his ministry. After his resurrection from the dead, he was with his disciples to continue unfolding the meaning of Holy Scripture: "Then he said to them, 'These are my words that I spoke to you while I was still with you—that everything written about me in the law of Moses, the prophets, and the psalms must be fulfilled.' Then he opened their minds to understand the scriptures..." (Luke 24:44-45).

Jesus' disciples still sit at his feet in order to hear him explain the meaning of the ancient writings. The division of our Bibles into "Old Testament" and "New Testament" is not arbitrary and serves an important purpose. The former anticipates the latter, and the new opens vistas for us in the wake of Jesus' life, ministry, death, and resurrection that are not available in the old. But we must not make the mistake of trying to read the New Testament apart from the Old Testament. There is a radical continuity in Scripture.

To anyone who wonders why it matters to Christians what the Hebrew Bible says on the subject, I would reply first by stressing what I have just called the "radical continuity" of the Word of God. The space devoted in previous chapters of this book to exploring Old Testament teaching on divorce was necessary for all that will follow. The words of Jesus and Paul on the subject presume that content. What Jesus said is made far more intelligible when one knows the texts he is citing, interpreting, and applying. Second, I would insist that anything Jesus or Paul says on the subject must be consistent with the Old Testament material, for Holy Scripture is progressive revelation—from partial to full, but never from error to truth. That is, I believe that the teachings in our canonical New Testament are to be interpreted with a view toward their continuity with the Old Testament. Scripture in its totality is God-breathed, and God's character as a being of maximal holiness and love has not changed from the days of Abraham and David to the time of Jesus and Paul.

As we begin to read and interpret the words of Jesus directly, it will be important to keep them in their historical and cultural setting. We must not force a meaning on Scripture that it could not have had for its original hearers. We sometimes err with good intentions when we read the Gospel of Matthew as if it were written to our time and place or reflects our social institutions and habits. Just as the teachings of Torah emerged from a particular set of circumstances and addressed the needs of people facing them, so do the teachings of Jesus. It is not always easy to determine the original setting of biblical statements, but difficulty does not free us from responsibility.

It is very important, for example, to know that the divorce and remarriage statements of the Old Testament were given to regulate and improve existing cultural practices and not to create divorce. And we know enough of the circumstances of the Ancient Near East into which the Mosaic statutes were introduced that we can be certain that remarriage was always presumed to be one's right following divorce. Scripture presumes the same thing, and there was no need for the Old Testament to specify circumstances under which a second marriage was allowed. Anyone who was legally divorced had the right to marry again. Thus a text such as Deuteronomy 24:1ff presumes a divorced woman's right to remarriage and protected her from both personal slander and the appropriation of her property. In the patriarchal culture of the time, divorce was actually a Mosaic means of defending otherwise abandoned women and protecting them from future exploitation. A man might divorce his wife and send her from his home to fend for herself in other cultures of that time, but the women of Israel could not be treated with such cavalier contempt for their personhood and dignity.

There are still several regions of our world where laws and customs are little different from the cultural practices that were in place in the time of Abraham or Moses. A few years back, I read with intense interest a newspaper story about the longstanding history of low status and ill treatment of women in countries such as Afghanistan.[12] It told the horrifying story of a 20-year-old woman who was recovering from a suicide attempt. She had doused herself with kerosene and set herself on fire. It was an incident that human rights workers in that country said was typical of hundreds of such cases each year.

The woman was given by her family into an arranged marriage to a man much older than her. In the home of her new extended family, she began to be mistreated and beaten. "All the time they beat me," she said. "They broke my arm. But what should I do? This was my home."

A deputy minister of women's affairs for the Afghanistan government admitted that abuse of the sort the woman described for the press was behind many suicides each year. "Some take tablets. Some cut their wrists. Some hang themselves. Some burn themselves," she told the reporter. "But the reason is very important. The first reason is our very bad tradition of forced marriage. Girls think this is the only way, that there is no other way in life."

Stories of this sort make me more acutely aware of the cruelties human beings can inflict on one another. It highlights the mistreatment women are forced to endure in many cultures. And it gives a context from which one is able to understand and appreciate the protection that was intended to follow from the Old Testament's "certificate of divorce" that men had to give the wives they chose to reject.

Some who denigrate the Bible for its "oppression of women" would be wise to study a number of biblical texts within their cultural setting before making an altogether negative case against Judeo-Christian Scripture.

Far from being harsh and unfair, various provisions in the Pentateuch were meant to protect Jewish women. If their husbands did divorce them, they had to provide a document certifying the divorce and granting the woman her freedom to marry another man. The economic importance of this procedure was no less important. A woman's divorce certificate meant that any future prosperity she experienced upon returning to her family of origin or through her remarriage would be shielded from any claims by her first husband. After all, if the man she once lived with was coldhearted enough to put her out of his house and life, it would not be beyond him to reclaim "his property" at some later time. Torah essentially said that women are not property or animals but must be treated as persons with rights. This information will be crucial for the interpretation of what Jesus is recorded to have said in Matthew 19.

As further evidence of the continuity between Old Testament and New Testament teachings about divorce, Jesus explicitly said at Matthew 5:17-20 that he did not intend to abrogate (i.e., rescind, disallow, annul) the Law of Moses but to fulfill (i.e., satisfy, comply with, complete) it.

When one has been careful to be as responsible as possible in studying these ancient texts, he must finally draw conclusions as to how the laws, insights, and principles discovered there apply to the cultural circumstances of our own time and place. Someone who is enamored of "objectivity" and determined to establish a "formula" for deciding difficult cases may claim to discern a fixed, immutable law for deciding who may or may not divorce. He may fix the degree of justification required for those who seek to divorce under that law. He may decide who may—or must not—consider remarriage as an option after divorce. He may even prescribe what to do with anyone whose situation contravenes the law as he has articulated it. On the other hand, some may feel free either to bypass the labor of serious Bible study or to ignore the results of it for the sake of encouraging "personal authenticity" or "radical freedom." These are, of course, caricatures of the most extreme sort. Very few people who would bother with a book such as this one can be fairly represented through such distortions.

Neither of these extreme approaches to the matter of divorce and remarriage is ultimately helpful to someone who affirms Scripture to be inspired of God in its origin and normative for the lives of Christ's disciples in its application. My life situation is not the same as Abraham's, and my wife could not understand or live that of his wife, Sarah. For that matter, she and I do not live in the much-changed-from-Abraham's-time culture of Jesus of Nazareth. But we are not free to cut ourselves off from the things God revealed of his nature and will in the earlier act of the drama being played out on the stage of Planet Earth.

Therefore, when I speak of applying the insights and principles discovered in rigorous Bible study to our time and place, I must confess a degree of subjectivity. The subjectivity of which I speak is hardly that of "pulling ideas out of the blue" in order to think, teach, or act as I please. It is a Spirit-guided and community-oriented subjectivity that is always bounded by the authority of Scripture. I believe the Holy Spirit who saw to the giving of the Word of God is continually at work to make that word "living and active" for the ongoing life of God's people (cf. Heb 4:12). The community within whose safety and nurture Holy Scripture is best explored and where one's conclusions may be subjected to scrutiny is the church.

Because Scripture is not an end in itself, however, the central interpretive norm for the Spirit-filled community of faith is Jesus. This chapter is therefore particularly important to this book. It seeks to delineate and apply Jesus' way of reading Scripture as the model by which we should read the Hebrew Bible. It also seeks to hear any new teaching he brings within the flow of progressive revelation from the Father. And it seeks not only for understandings that match those of Jesus but for the ability to deal with persons who have failed either to understand or to live his correct understandings with his healing grace.

Sermon on the Mount: Our "Interpretive Key"

In my opinion, the single most instructive place for hearing Jesus on the matter of divorce and remarriage is the Sermon on the Mount. Although Matthew 19 is a longer text and is specifically set in the context of interpreting Old Testament statements about divorce and remarriage, Matthew 5-7 provides an instructive environment for grasping how Jesus read Scripture and understood its authority to function. It therefore provides a hermeneutical reference point for interpreting all his sayings, including the other Gospel statements from him about divorce and remarriage.

Matthew's Sermon on the Mount revolves around this paragraph:

> Do not think that I have come to abolish the law or the prophets; I have come not to abolish but to fulfill. For truly I tell you, until heaven and earth pass away, not one letter, not one stroke of a letter, will pass from the law until all is accomplished. Therefore, whoever breaks one of the least of these commandments, and teaches others to do the same, will be called least in the kingdom of heaven; but whoever does them and teaches them will be called great in the kingdom of heaven. For I tell you, unless your righteousness exceeds that of the scribes and Pharisees, you will never enter the kingdom of God. (Matt 5:17-20)

Without wanting to be unfair to the scribes and Pharisees of the time and while not assuming there were no exceptions to the rule (cf. Nicodemus, John 3:1ff), Jesus' encounters with them in our canonical

Gospels reflects a community of religious fundamentalists who were committed to careful scholarship, preservation of Judaic orthodoxy, and enforcement of ritual purity. During the period of their intense and ongoing conflict with Jesus, they were typically held in high regard by their peers. They were serious about Scripture. They wanted to be "separated"—the basic meaning of the word Pharisee—from all things that would defile. But their ultra-conservative and highly restrictive views often put them in situations where they became liable to Jesus' charge of spiritual hypocrisy. The Pharisees and scribes had been caught in the trap that has ensnared so many of us at one point or another. Trying to take God's words seriously, they wound up creating a performance model for righteousness. On that model, righteousness was centered on deciphering Scripture and holding oneself and others to the most scrupulous observance of divine law in every detail—while "missing the point" about loving God and loving neighbor.

The problem with a performance model that builds on doctrinal correctness coupled with inflexible lifestyle conformity to all the demands of biblical morality is that one can never "get it right." Am I quite sure that my interpretation is correct beyond the possibility of error? If so, how should I treat those who are wrong? If not, what is the point of serious study of Scripture? How well do I measure up to the things I know with such certainty? How can I be quiet when others do not measure up to those holy standards? Must I not separate myself from those who fall short of holiness in order to maintain my own integrity? Will this approach tend to make me not only fussy and legalistic in my own handling of Scripture but also highly judgmental of others?

Even if all this sounds familiar to some of us, doesn't it sound strange to put such a works-based system into words? Doesn't it sound wearisome? Among other things, this model represents God as the keeper of a great balance sheet on every human life and tends to drive its adherents into ever-narrowing contexts for positive human interaction and camaraderie. For the sake of perfect separation from all that defiles, one judges piety mostly in terms of the evil he shuns rather than the goodness and joy he radiates. Over a period of time, the system makes one increasingly angry, critical, and isolated.

Perhaps the widespread high regard for this performance model of good religion in his day is what shocked so many people about Jesus. He was gregarious and outgoing. He included children and women, Samaritans and Gentiles, even those who collected taxes for the unclean Roman occupiers. He greeted and treated with respect persons who were known to walk the streets to ply their unholy trade in human flesh. An upright religionist—whose perceived duty was to separate from evil— might cry, "Away with the unclean!" Jesus looked at the same people and said, "Follow me!" So what could this unsettling rabbi have meant by saying, "Be *perfect*, therefore, as your heavenly Father is perfect"? (Matt 5:48).

The perfection envisioned in the Sermon on the Mount requires that one reject the performance model of the scribes and Pharisees for the sake of a personal relationship with Jesus as the one who came to fulfill all that was anticipated in the Law and the Prophets. It is this *fulfillment motif* that is so critical to interpreting not only the Sermon on the Mount but the larger role of Jesus in the drama of Holy Scripture. It involves far more than the simplistic apologetics formula of prediction and implementation. He was not claiming merely that he had satisfied the predictions about a virgin giving birth at Bethlehem or a dead person being restored to life. Oh, he did. And the completion of those prophetic anticipations is crucial to establishing Jesus as the long-awaited Messiah of Israel. But he was so much more. He "accomplishes" or "fulfills" the Law and the Prophets by going infinitely beyond what they could communicate.

> Contrary to the opinion of some, [Matt] 5:20 does not demand a more rigorous keeping of the Law or a more rigorous interpretation of the Law. Rather, Jesus, according to Matthew, demands a *righteousness* congruent with his coming. *Righteousness* necessary for entrance into the Kingdom connotes the conduct in keeping with the will of the Father, conduct that stems from the new relationships and possibilities inherent in the presence of the age of salvation and implicit in

the demands of 5:21–7:12. The *righteousness of the scribes and Pharisees* was inadequate because it did not stem from the eschatological moment of God's redemptive activity in Jesus' Messianic ministry, restoring the broken relationships between himself and his people as well as among his people, enabling them to live in keeping with his will.[13]

The Law and the Prophets had pointed for centuries before the birth of Jesus to someone who would come in God's good time. He would be greater than Moses (Deut 18:15-18) and would write the words of God directly on human hearts rather than on stone tablets (Jer 31:31-34). The Messiah would put a "new spirit" within those who were seeking God that would enable them to live out the divine decrees whose goal was righteousness (Ezek 36:25-27). This would not be a prediction-to-accomplishment formula but something quite different. God's Chosen One would "accomplish" what laws and statutes could not and "fulfill" the divine longing for human righteousness in himself. Thus the New Testament presents Jesus as the one who went above and beyond what law could do or create in us. It then presents his gracious offer of a new kind or quality of righteousness that all who come to him could receive as a free gift—one the scribes and Pharisees had missed on account of their preoccupation with the minutiae of commandments.

The difference between Jesus and the Pharisees was that Jesus read the Law of Moses relationally and they read it legally. Or, as some have expressed it, Jesus read Torah prophetically in the midst of people accustomed to reading it casuistically (i.e., as legal stipulations whose performance conferred right standing). By his approach, Jesus was standing in the tradition of such prophetic interpreters of Torah as Isaiah and Amos. Seven centuries before the birth of Jesus, they were part of a prophetic chorus already trying to get the Chosen People to embrace a piety that went beyond mere religious formality. While not disparaging the Law, worship rituals, or mandatory sacrifices, they challenged the people to look beyond the technical requirements of Torah to the healthy relationships those rules sought to foster. Thus we find language such as this:

> I hate, I despise your festivals,
>> and I take no delight in your solemn assemblies.
> Even though you offer me your burnt offerings and grain offerings,
>> I will not accept them;
> and the offerings of well-being of your fatted animals
>> I will not look upon.
> Take away from me the noise of your songs;
>> I will not listen to the melody of your harps.
> But let justice roll down like waters,
>> and righteousness like an ever-flowing stream.
>> (Amos 5:21-24)

Neither Amos nor Matthew nor Jesus is to be heard as disparaging the Law or dismissing any of its holy requirements. Instead, we should hear them saying that no stipulation of any biblical law ought to be used to evade or substitute for that document's clear intention. The laws were given in their entirety to help define, protect, and enhance human relationships with their God and among themselves. Thus the laws about festivals, for example, had to be read in terms not only of day, time, and proper ritual but the well-being of the worshiping community.

Heard as a moralist's diatribe, the Sermon on the Mount is an impossible-to-bear judgment. Read as a series of mandates for Jesus' disciples, it is an impossible-to-attain standard. Heard as heaven's dream for the creatures made in God's own image, however, the sermon becomes an impossible-to-wait-for world of Eden restored. Read as the Heavenly Father's reality in which we participate as his children by being transformed into the likeness of the one Perfect Son, it is our new-creation identity dawning on us and forming in our daily life habits. This is a righteousness that both fulfills the Law and the Prophets and exceeds that of the scribes and Pharisees.

In this new paradigm for righteousness, we experience what could not be fathomed at some earlier act in the drama. Ever see one of those old black-and-white Western movies? The ones I have in mind are the *really* old ones—pre-John Wayne and the shoot-'em-up sheriffs. The first few minutes show what happens when there is no law. People fight and steal and plot their revenge. Violence breeds more violence, and there is neither safety nor civility. Then the stranger in a white hat arrives in town. There is no doubt of his strength and toughness, but he has no drive to "mow people down." He is secure in himself, and his presence begins to change the expectations of others. In the central plot, he doesn't kill the bad guy but wins him over. He helps him see options he has feared to try, for he had never seen them modeled. With his authority established now, the hero posts a few signs and publishes the laws that allow people to walk the streets, open their shops for business, fall in love, and rear their children. The movie ends with a blissful scene in which violence has given way not simply to civil order but to idyllic serenity. The wide-open town of lawless brigands has become a veritable paradise. That story line in a variety of contexts was popular in theater fantasies because it is the dream we human beings carry in our hearts for our own place in the cosmos. The only true implementation of that desire, however, is in what the Bible calls the Kingdom of God.

When the Fall left Planet Earth reeling in its lawlessness, moral chaos, and depravity, life itself was insecure and insignificant. People not only abused one another in violent acts but with social institutions such as slavery and widespread abuse of women. God sent Moses and other righteous spokesmen to decry our wholesale departure from his initial plan for human life in Eden. Mighty acts in history established the authority of his prophets, and more than once he attacked evil with flood, plague, or sword. Laws were given from Sinai and published at a variety of times and places to curb the most brutal and excessive of actions. But even the prophets who posted the laws and called the people to heed them looked past the minimal state of affairs law could ever hope to establish to a time when Messiah would appear, usher in the Kingdom of God, and bring about what compliance to statutes could not. So Jesus came—not to judge the world but to redeem it. He didn't purge the world with violence but absorbed its death-blows in his own body. He told his disciples to spread the seed of the kingdom, to water and nurture the tender growth, and to pray for the kingdom to come for all. If such a day were to come, it would be like the one in which you could expect to see lions and lambs lie down beside one another without fear.

Put in terms of events I have witnessed with my own eyes, we would know the Kingdom of God is among us when an adult child visits a prison, sits with the man who murdered his mother, and forgives him. We are experiencing God's reign over human hearts when a family receives a guilt-burdened man in a hospital's burn unit where their child is unconscious and fighting for his life because of that man's error. They receive him there in order to say, "We release you from the burden you are carrying over this and are praying for your heart to heal—just as we are praying for our son's life to be spared and for him to heal from his injuries." The kingdom is on display when a woman both confronts and forgives her childhood molester. The Kingdom of God is also in view when a man receives at his daughter's wedding the mother who abandoned the family for another man, and then forgives, leads their daughter through the beginnings of a family reconciliation, and graciously includes the woman and her second husband in the events of the wedding.

Marvin and Sue married the summer following their graduation from college. Sue grew up in a Christian home where love was modeled by devout believers, and Marvin accepted Christ in the spring of his sophomore year—shortly after he and Sue had started dating. They received counseling from the minister who officiated their wedding and were fully committed to making their life together a holy experience until death separated them.

During 23 years of marriage, they had two children. Sue worked as an elementary school teacher, and Marvin created his own CPA firm. They were active in their church as Bible School teachers. Both were highly respected in the city. And their children seemed well-adjusted and happy.

People could not have known what was happening during those two decades. It was not a "bad marriage" with any of the presenting problems of infidelity, abuse, or alcoholism. It was a "good marriage" often neglected. She was busy with school and children; he was focused on building his business. Even when they took "family time," it was for the children's plays, athletics, and church events.

Marvin and Sue simply became strangers to each other. A year after the younger child left home for college, everyone was shocked—including their children!—when Sue filed for divorce. "We just drifted apart," she told their friends. Marvin agreed and said, "We will always care about each other, and both of us will be there for the children. We just forgot to pay attention to each other—and let our love die."

Life moved on. Both children graduated from college. Both married. Both continued to have positive contact with both of their parents. Then, seven and a half years after the divorce, Marvin began dating a woman who had recently moved to his hometown. Her husband of almost 30 years had died three years ago, and she had come back to take care of her ailing mother. After her mother died of Alzheimer's Disease, she hired Marvin to sort out the family estate, tax documents, and other financial matters.

Their courtship began when Marvin asked Joyce to go to lunch with him after they had worked hard in his office one morning on some estate issues. With more still to be done, he suggested they grab a quick bite and come back to finish. That meal and its casual conversation about family and faith let them know they had much in common. They were both lonely, and it was obvious to both that they would enjoy spending time together. Joyce also has two grown children and one grandchild, and her Christian faith has always been central to her life.

You are one of Marvin's best friends. You always have him in your home for your annual Christmas party. Will the events of this past year change anything for you? If Marvin and Joyce get engaged in October, does that change anything? What if they get married on Thanksgiving Day?

The mistake so many of us have made over time has been to read the Sermon on the Mount as good Pharisees and to debate it as pedantic scribes. But Jesus intended from the beginning for his apprentices in kingdom living to pursue righteousness along a different path. What he called righteousness that "exceeds" (NRSV) or "surpasses" (NIV) that of the scribes and Pharisees is relational rather than formal. That is, it requires us to respect and apply the laws we know in light of the principles they reflect and for the sake of the redemptive purpose of the loving God who gave them. Thus his treatment, for example, of the sabbath that brought him into conflict with many. Yet his insistence that "The sabbath was made for humankind, and not humankind for the sabbath" is not only about what his disciples should do on Saturdays but models a way of reading every rule, statute, and law in Scripture. *Biblical law is to be interpreted through its original divine intention to bless, humanize, and empower people and not for the purpose of making their lives hopelessly complex and difficult.*

Dallas Willard is correct when he writes:

> [W]e need to put the idea of *laws* entirely out of our minds. Jesus is working... at the much deeper level of the *source* of actions, good and bad. He is taking us deeper into the kind of beings we are, the kind of love God has for us, and the kind of love that, as we share it, brings us into harmony with his life. No one can be "right" in the kingdom sense who is not transformed at this level. And then, of course, the issue of *not* being wrongly angry, *not* expressing contempt, *not* calling people [fools], and so on is automatically taken care of.[14]

The purpose of every divine stipulation—whether written on stone tablets or into the intuitive consciousness of every human being—has been to liberate people to be what God always intended us to be. God's holy purpose is not to enslave his creatures with rules but to free us from things that would otherwise keep us from loving him and one another as we should. The way many of Jesus' contemporaries were using Torah was having the opposite effect of making people brittle, harsh, and judgmental with one another. They had turned law into an end in itself—more concerned for actions than attitudes, reputation than character, externals than internals. In the Sermon on the Mount, Jesus calls us back to heaven's original intent. He points to the path that is whole-heart, whole-life discipleship that reaches to the depths of our personalities and beings.

Matthew 5:31-32

Nowhere is it harder to keep the nature and purpose of the Sermon on the Mount clearly in mind than in these two verses. We are so accustomed to parsing them in good Pharisaic style that—even while warning against being legalistic with them—we tend inevitably to run to them with the wrong questions and thus end up arguing for the wrong answers. Stassen and Gushee, for example, contend that a hefty contingent of evangelical biblical scholars has tended to "reflect a highly legalistic approach" to questions of Christian ethics generally because of a mistaken beginning point.

> They focus on rules and exceptions rather than the character of God, scriptural principles that reflect that character, real human situations that reflect our bondage to sin, and transformative practices. They tend to ask the permissibility questions: *Under what circumstances is it morally permissible to get divorced or remarried?* Is it permissible for a divorced person to serve as a minister? Should a minister participate in marrying someone who has been divorced? They demonstrate little sensitivity to the human context in which all Christian ethics is done. What results is moral teaching torn asunder from contact with human experience, sometimes culminating in irrelevance or even cruelty.[15]

In his commentary on the Pentateuch, Jesus consistently offers his apprentices in spiritual living a new way to read and interpret Scripture that abandons the performance model in favor of a relational model. So Jesus takes up a series of six statements or commandments from Torah in order to explain them relationally. He explains laws about murder, adultery, divorce, oath-taking, retaliation, and the treatment of one's neighbors. In none of these cases is he contrasting falsehood with truth or even Old Testament versus New Testament. Instead, he contrasts the interpretation commonly being taught in his day with what God had been trying to do in Scripture. He was setting the performance model of the scribes and Pharisees over against the heart of God for the people accountable to him. He was telling his apprentices the difference in law as statute and law as grace and truth.

Jesus was neither the first nor the last rabbi to use a formula comparable to the one here: "You have heard *this*, but I tell you *that*." We do something similar when we say or hear this: "The way you've heard the Bible explained on this point is this, but I am convinced that it really means that." But Jesus' formula needs to be understood in even stronger terms— not, I remind you, contrasting either Moses with himself or what we call the Old Testament with the New Testament. "You have had God's will on murder or oaths or adultery interpreted this way," he was saying, "but the 'fulfillment' of Scripture on that point is much deeper and fuller." And the ultimate mistake in our hearing or reading his commentary is to take it to be still another layer of law on top of law already in place.

After speaking first to the issues of murder (vs. 21-26) and adultery (vs. 27-30), Jesus raises the subject of divorce:

> It was also said, "Whoever divorces his wife, let him give her a certificate of divorce. But I say to you that anyone who divorces his wife, except on the ground of unchastity, causes her to commit adultery; and whoever marries a divorced woman commits adultery."

First, on a legalistic reading, the only person who doesn't sin in this text is the person who is the root of the problem. That is, the "adultery" indictments in this text are only for the defenseless woman who is sent away and the poor fellow who later marries her—not for the heartless cad who initially divorces her. Second, such a reading of these two verses means that Jesus abolished the protection of women created by Deuteronomy 24. Third, it ignores the obvious hyperbole at work in this section that makes hatred as bad as murder (v. 22) and lust equivalent to adultery (v. 28).

It is just such Christian legalism in reading this section of the Sermon on the Mount that has forced Christian teachers and whole churches to adopt unjustifiably strict rules forbidding remarriage after divorce—while missing the point of Jesus altogether. For example, the Anglican Church does not allow people to remarry following divorce. And that presented the late C. S. Lewis a problem in relation to the divorced American he loved, Joy Gresham. They were married in a private civil ceremony in April of 1956, but the blessing of the church was important to both of them. Whether Lewis believed it necessary or simply conceded to the rules of the church, I cannot say. But he did something I have seen repeated many times in my own tradition. He reasoned his way to a loophole in the legalistic interpretation of Jesus' words—and jumped through it.

> Apparently, Lewis argued that because Bill Gresham had been married before he married Joy, and his first wife was still living, their marriage was not a true Christian marriage. An old pupil of Lewis, the Reverend Peter Bide, agreed and married them at Joy's bedside at the Churchill Hospital at Oxford on April 21, 1957.[16]

Reading his words in context and without the nuances of forced legalism, it is possible to know what Jesus meant here. Just walk through the commandments about murder, adultery, and divorce.

First, if scribal legalism had said one is innocent of murder until he takes the life of the person he hates, the ethic of the Kingdom of God says that walking the path of hatred and vilification of another human being is forbidden; not just the taking of an enemy's life but a person's unwillingness to seek reconciliation with an enemy is offensive to God. So the commandment "You shall not murder" must be interpreted to mean that Christ's disciples are never to justify hatred, malign people, or otherwise foster the disruption of human community. For the purpose of being pure in heart and a peacemaker, it is the very first step on hatred's path—and not just the final step of taking a life—that makes one a lawbreaker and "liable to the hell of fire." Jesus overstated his case and used hyperbole to make his point.

Second, if the Pharisees had taught (or even implied) that lecherous males were deemed faithful to their wives so long as they were not guilty of extramarital sex, "Jesus demanded a relationship between men and women that not only outlawed the physical act of adultery but also the adulterous thought."[17] Remember the field day the American press had when then-candidate Jimmy Carter said he had been guilty of "adultery in [his] heart" on occasion? That type of reaction to the issue of lust is not only Pharisaical but sexist and demeaning to human dignity. But that is precisely the point Jesus was trying to make. Anyone who has a transformed, born-from-above heart doesn't see how close he or she can get to "crossing the line" but is horrified by even the slightest prompting in the direction of doing so.

Third, if the throng around Jesus had heard it said that issuing the appropriate certificate made divorce acceptable under biblical teachings, the Son of Man was bold to declare that divorce and remarriage constitute adultery. The essence of marriage is not a dowry, legal document, or ceremony; it is pledging and keeping faith with another. Similarly, the horror of divorce is not that some people fail to execute the divorce certificate; it is that anyone would break faith with his (or her) mate by abandoning a covenant commitment. Jesus' half-brother was apparently so struck by the force of this reasoning that he wrote—likely drawing on both Jesus' words here and the Yahweh-Israel relationship of the Old Testament—that any Christian who breaks faith with God by compromising his fidelity to Christ is guilty of adultery. "Adulterers! Do you not know that friendship with the world is enmity with God?" (Jas 4:4a).

Jesus did not trump and abolish Deuteronomy 24:1-4 by means of his words in Matthew 5:31-32. He did not replace the existing Old Testament divorce and remarriage statute with a more restrictive New Testament edict. For the sake of anyone who would hear him, he spoke with conspicuous exaggeration to call attention to a new kind of righteousness that exceeds the legalism of scribes and Pharisees—whether ancient or modern. Jesus was not, in fact, giving a new piece of legislation here. To the contrary, he was attempting to help us understand the deeper meaning, original intent, or kingdom fulfillment of the statements already found in Scripture. Remember: the progressive revelation of Holy Scripture is never from error to truth but from partial to complete. If law had been given long before to ameliorate some of the harsh and ungodly chaos that was causing humans to hurt and destroy one another, the ideal state God has always dreamed of for his human creatures was to be embraced by those who confess Jesus as their Lord. Instead of figuring out the loopholes for divorce and remarriage, let us instead look for ways to make our lives and relationships—especially the covenant relationship of marriage—holy.

Yet the embracing of this kingdom ideal does not mean that no more marriages will fail because they have been formed hastily by immature souls who lack the ability to provide the companionship, nurture, and love their vows pledged. It does not mean that someone who does have those abilities won't be deceived by someone who is angling merely for security, social standing, or money—but who now is indissolubly bound to that person so long as he or she is not sexually promiscuous.

The idea that a woman would sin to divorce a man who beats her—so long as he hasn't slept with someone else—seems outrageous. Similarly, the idea that a man who reluctantly divorces a woman who is a chronic alcoholic and who is neglecting and endangering their children is offending God sounds equally absurd. Or perhaps someone's position is that such persons could divorce but have to remain single and celibate after that divorce—lest they be guilty of adultery. These notions simply do not square with the biblical materials. And the use of the Bible either to imprison people in unholy relationships or to deny them the freedom to move on with life as forgiven people in search of wholeness is every bit as irresponsible as the cavalier attitude of those who dismiss marriage altogether as trivial, nothing more than "legalized prostitution," or an archaic holdover from a time that no longer is.

Remember the case study earlier in this chapter involving Marvin and Sue? Do you remember the marriage scenario involving Marvin's later marriage to a woman named Joyce? (If not, please flip back a few pages and review it before reading further.) If you read that case and answered that Marvin and Joyce would commit adultery by marrying, be living in adultery, and be married only under human statutes and not in God's sight, then add the following to it:

Seventeen months after Marvin and Joyce got married, Marvin and Sue's older child was in a near-fatal car wreck while away on business in Toronto. Marvin and Sue both rushed there and agonized for days as their child underwent three major surgeries. Now he would be in the hospital's ICU for an indefinite period of time. They took rooms at the same motel across the street from the hospital. It wasn't in the best part of town, and Marvin saw to it that his former wife was safely in her room at the end of each exhausting day.

As their other child, Joyce, and several mutual friends came in and out of the hospital, Marvin and Sue relived memories of their injured son's life. The plays, soccer games, Little League, experimentation with cigarettes—a thousand things came back to mind. The conversations seemed to take them back across the years. They were both surprised and confused by some of the feelings that were stirred in them by their rich, multi-layered memories.

One evening they were at the hospital alone. No friends had come that afternoon. Joyce had gone back home to get some additional clothes for her and Marvin. Alone together now for the first time in years, Marvin and Sue began talking about their now-improved son's first date. They laughed about his awkwardness with the girl he took to see the G-Rated movie they had picked and approved for that evening. They continued to talk and both teared up a bit as they reached Sue's room. Their own flesh and blood had nearly died on an ice-slick highway and was still in critical condition just across the street. It seemed so unreal. Sue asked that they pray together for his recovery.

So Marvin entered Sue's room, and the two of them dropped to their knees. Holding hands, both parents prayed fervently for their son. Then they held each other as they sobbed out the tensions and fears of the past few days. Then they kissed. And in a matter of minutes they were undressed and in Sue's bed—where Marvin spent the rest of the night. When he woke up the next morning, he looked at Sue and asked himself, "What have we done?"

What is your answer? If they are "still married in the eyes of God," it would appear they did nothing immoral. If they committed sin that night, however, it would seem that Marvin must really be married (in God's eyes as well as under human statute) to Joyce.

Should Marvin divorce Joyce and try to put things back together with Sue? (Remember that this is what Deuteronomy 24:1-4 explicitly forbids.) Or should he repent of his tryst with Sue and renew good faith with Joyce?

The tendency of some is to take Jesus' challenge to Pharisaic and scribal legalism and to transform it into an even narrower, stricter, and more legalistic reading of the Pentateuch. What irony! That is, there are some who read Jesus to be saying: "Yes, under the Law of Moses a marriage could be terminated and all the parties involved would be permitted—even expected—to marry again. But now marriages are never to be terminated. Henceforth, if such a thing were to happen, no one can be permitted to marry again—with the solitary exception of the one 'innocent party' who has kept his or her vows faithfully, only to be betrayed by an unfaithful spouse. And that is the meaning of law giving way to grace." A non-contextual reading of Jesus' statements in the Sermon on the Mount may permit such a view, but the words of Jesus in their historical setting and against the background of Old Testament would never have been understood this way.

CHAPTER FIVE

JESUS ON DIVORCE AND REMARRIAGE PART 2

In the previous chapter, we traced some implications of Jesus' way of reading Scripture. With the sabbath commandment, for example, it means understanding sabbath as blessing rather than curse, permission to enjoy God rather than burdensome impositions from God. In the Sermon on the Mount, Jesus looked at Old Testament precepts about murder, adultery, and the "certificate of divorce" by that method. In this chapter, we move to his discussion of divorce and remarriage in Matthew 19 and draw some conclusions from his teaching.

Jesus interpreted all the desires of God for the humans created in his image in light of what he called the two great commandments—love God with your whole being and love your neighbor as yourself. In reading Scripture for our time and place, this positioning of ourselves to read the biblical commandments as reflections of love and grace remains all-important. The failure to do so makes us into modern-day equivalents of the Pharisees and scribes who were so often set against Jesus.

In the previous chapter we saw Jesus' use of preaching rhetoric to tease his hearers to thoughtful reflection. Thus, hatred is murder, lust is adultery, and divorce causes the person put away to be adulterated. (I know that

reading "to be adulterated" is awkward, but the verb Jesus chose was a passive verb—not "to commit adultery" but "to be adulterated.") This is
hyperbole. It is obvious exaggeration for the sake of emphasis. Don't
indulge anger and lust, for these impulses can sweep *you* onto a path that
leads to destruction. And don't put away your companion, for that action
can put *her* life into a tailspin that thwarts heaven's plan for her holiness.

In none of these situations was Jesus trying to "tighten the screws" on
people, as if that would eliminate unrighteous behaviors. He did not take
the attainable prohibition against murder and ratchet it up to an impossi-
ble-to-obey command against anger. Neither may we reasonably understand him to teach that lust is as bad as adultery. Yet we have succumbed
to the mistake of equating divorce and remarriage with adultery. Anger,
lust, and failure to stay married may all be repented of and forgiven. And
the fruits of repentance in all three of these cases demand not an undoing
of the past but a determination to handle stresses and temptations differently in the future. If divorce and remarriage are different from hatred and
lust in this regard, how can that be?

Jesus and his disciples walk the fine line between demanding that
cruel, intolerable, and spiritually destructive marriages be maintained at
all costs and appearing to give people permission to walk away from
covenant commitments that Scripture says must be honored. But is that
really a "fine line"? Is a man whose wife kills their children by drowning
them in a bathtub sentenced—along with her sentence either to prison or
a mental hospital—to remain single until he dies? Does a woman whose
husband is sentenced to prison for life for habitual criminal behavior have
no recourse but to remain married to him? Or may she divorce him so long
as she stays unmarried? There does not seem to be a fine line between
these souls and a "serial marrier" in Hollywood; I would more nearly say
the situations are light years apart.

Matthew 19:1-9

A more extensive engagement with the subject of divorce and remarriage
than his brief comments in the Sermon on the Mount is found later in the

Gospel of Matthew. The setting here is different from that of Matthew 5. Jesus is not making statements about marriage and divorce but is challenged by some of the very Pharisees whose way of dealing with Scripture he had stood on its head. Realistically, they had surely heard of his teaching. So we are to understand this context as one of challenge to the upstart rabbi who had said they were missing the heart of God's will on this important subject.

> When Jesus had finished saying these things, he left Galilee and went to the region of Judea beyond the Jordan. Large crowds followed him, and he cured them there.
> Some Pharisees came to him, and to test him they asked, "Is it lawful for a man to divorce his wife for any cause?" He answered, "Have you not read that the one who made them at the beginning 'made them male and female', and said, 'For this reason a man shall leave his father and mother and be joined to his wife, and the two shall become one flesh'? So they are no longer two, but one flesh. Therefore what God has joined together, let no one separate." They said to him, "Why then did Moses command us to give a certificate of dismissal and to divorce her?" He said to them, "It was because you were so hard-hearted that Moses allowed you to divorce your wives, but at the beginning it was not so. And I say to you, whoever divorces his wife, except for unchastity, and marries another commits adultery."
> His disciples said to him, "If such is the case of a man with his wife, it is better not to marry." But he said to them, "Not everyone can accept this teaching, but only those to whom it is given. For there are eunuchs who have been so from birth, and there are eunuchs who have been made eunuchs by others, and there are eunuchs who have made themselves eunuchs for the sake of the kingdom of heaven. Let anyone accept this who can."

In examining this text, we must keep a few things in mind that help in its interpretation. First, this challenge to Jesus did not happen in a theological-cultural vacuum. We can understand what is happening here only if we have an idea of the issue at stake in the conversation. Second, Jesus answered the question put to him in this text in light of his agenda rather than that of his critics. That is, he did not get into the Pharisaic game of splitting hairs over this or that special circumstance but answered from his single-minded focus on establishing a moral vision that reflects the Kingdom of God. Third, readers at our distance from the conversation in question not only have to be very humble about interpreting what was said that day but must be even more cautious about lapsing back into legalism with the interpretation we derive. As we will see, Jesus never really told his questioners what to do about people who had taken divorce lightly and entered into marriages that never should have been formed, so we must be cautious about going beyond him in the counsel we give to such persons.

As to the context of the discussion, most Bible students are aware of the controversy raging in the time of Jesus between the competing interpretations of Rabbis Hillel and Shammai.[18] The former had insisted that the divorces envisioned in Deuteronomy 24:1-4 could be initiated for a variety of female offenses, ranging from adultery to flirting with men in public to burning her husband's meal; this lax view of divorce was dominant at the time, and it was common for men to divorce their wives "for any cause." The latter had argued that divorce should be pursued only in cases of sexual misconduct by a man's wife; this minority view of the time said that persons who divorced for trivial causes and then married again had done so in violation of Torah. It is interesting to note, however, that the Shammaites did not claim that such marriages were illegitimate in the sense that neither God nor man would recognize them. The second marriage was both holy and binding—so long as a certificate of divorce had been executed at the termination of the first marriage—but there was judged to be something dishonorable about the way the man had treated his original covenant marriage.

Knowing this much of the context for Matthew 19 helps us avoid the mistake of reading Jesus' words in a total vacuum. Yet there is additional information that helps still more. For one thing, we should read Jesus' injection of himself into the Hillelite-Shammaite debate with the awareness that their "issue" was not at all the issue at stake in Deuteronomy. In a previous chapter, it was pointed out that the legislation there appears to have had the singular goal of protecting women by making it impossible for men to reclaim their wives after a divorce. Deuteronomy 24 is *not* about reasons that would or would not justify divorce; it is a law put in place to protect the post-divorce rights of the woman. Over time and in good legalistic form, however, the discussion of this text came to focus not on the rights of women but on the circumstances under which men could divorce women.[19] What would constitute "something objectionable" (NRSV), "uncleanness" (KJV), an "unseemly thing" (ASV), or "indecency" (RSV) about a woman that could justify (?) a man in putting away his wife?

She spent time almost every day in Internet chat rooms. She later admitted to her attorney that she was "trolling for a big fish." She found him in the person of a middle-aged banker.

The man had limited personal skills. He was good with numbers and awkward with people. So he was flattered by the attention he was getting in the chat room from a woman seven years younger. If she was really as pretty as the pictures she had posted for him, he was going to be ecstatic and the envy of the men who had teased him for so long about being a bachelor.

They arranged to meet in Arizona to attend a weekend of spring training baseball games. He picked up the tab, and there were two rooms at the five-star hotel. He was a faithful church member and wasn't interested in sexual trysts. He wanted to meet someone, fall in love, and marry.

She had been willing to do whatever was necessary to move the relationship along. She didn't want to have sex with a "paunchy geezer" from the bank but was determined to do whatever was necessary to "reel him in."

There were three more weekend trips. Then she flew in to meet his family. And there was a big wedding seven weeks later.

The preacher who did their wedding ceremony didn't do premarital counseling. When he met with them about the wedding, he was shocked when he heard how they met, the speed of their courtship, and their rush to marry. His

*only comment was to say, "That's pretty fast, but I suppose you two are old
enough to know what you are doing."*

*Four months after the wedding, she was gone. She soon filed divorce papers
and asked for half the assets of a reasonably wealthy man.*

*Now he was back in the office of the minister who had officiated at his
wedding. "I was a fool and should have seen through it!" he said. "Now what
am I supposed to do?"*

In the chapters of this book that examined Old Testament teaching on
divorce, the meaning of "something objectionable" (Heb, *'erwat dabar*[20])
was not explored because it was an extraneous topic at that point. In the
earlier context, the only "law" at stake comes at the end of v.4 when a man
is forbidden to take back a woman he has disclaimed as a wife and sent
away. By the time of Jesus, however, the focus was precisely here and centered on the meaning of *'erwat dabar*. The school of Hillel argued that the
"something objectionable" could be essentially anything that displeased
the man of the house; the school of Shammai argued that the offense had
to be related to the man's exclusive sexual possession of his wife. Notice
that either interpretation is a movement away from the law's original purpose. In Matthew 19, some Pharisees showed up to "test" Jesus as to his
view of what the term signified.

Even so, the question as framed here is only about the meaning of a
disputed Hebrew term from Deuteronomy and not about the "legitimacy"
of divorces granted under other Old Testament provisions already noted.

When this tradition is read by itself, it would appear to suggest
that the Shammaites allowed divorce only on the grounds of adultery. However, we have seen above that the Shammaites also
accepted the three obligations of Exodus 21:10-11 [i.e., clothing,
food, conjugal rights] as valid grounds for divorce. Therefore,
although their words "a man may not divorce his wife unless he
finds indecency in her" appear at first glance to mean that divorce
could be *only* on the grounds of adultery, they cannot be read this

narrowly. The phrase should be understood in the context of the debate in which it is spoken, which was a debate about the meaning of Deuteronomy 24.[21]

Second, it is certainly obvious that Jesus replied to his questioners in this setting by appealing to a vision of God-human relationships in general, and marriage in particular, that surpassed that of his antagonists. He answered their specific question by siding with a stricter interpretation of the objectionable or indecent thing and limited justifiable divorce to "unchastity" (Gk, *porneia*). Then, consistent with what he had said in the Sermon on the Mount, he indicted men who divorced for trivial reasons as adulterers. Yet the real thrust of his answer was not to discuss divorce and remarriage but to appeal to the Edenic ideal of one man and one woman joined in loving commitment. "Therefore what God has joined together," he said, "let no one separate." In other words, separating husbands and wives from one another has never been the plan of God for marriage. Marriage in the manner of the Kingdom of God is a covenant commitment two people make and honor across time. The third issue of humility with our applications of Jesus' words here is always appropriate, no matter what issue of Christian doctrine and life is being studied.

When Jesus was approached and put to the test that day, his questioners apparently grasped that he would not have great sympathy for Rabbi Hillel's view. Thus we should probably read the question as "Is it lawful for a man to divorce his wife for (just) any cause" rather than "Is it (ever) lawful for a man to divorce his wife for any cause (whatsoever)"? (v.3) In other words, the context within which I grew up would have asked the question in its latter form. In attempting to follow Jesus in his high regard for marriage, we have stressed the inappropriateness of divorce to the degree that we questioned whether one should ever resort to it—even in the most extreme cases. Indeed, there are denominations that will not bless second marriages even when the so-called exception clause (i.e., "except for unchastity") is invoked and the affair has been admitted by the guilty party. That was *not* the issue put to Jesus that day. Everyone in Jesus' audience would have accepted that divorce in the case of sexual infidelity was appropriate, and many probably even considered it mandatory in such cases—as, perhaps, the "righteous man" Joseph did when he found that Mary was pregnant.

Thus the question is actually this: "Jesus, do you agree with the 'for any cause' approach to divorce?" Rather than be drawn directly into the old debate their question raised, his first response was not to settle divorce and remarriage questions but to affirm Yahweh's original intent for marriage as a one-flesh union that is never to be dissolved. As if to challenge their proof-texting from Deuteronomy, he appealed to Genesis and the divine plan for marriage "at the beginning" (vs.4-6).

Jesus' deft handling of the first question led his opponents to press a second one: "Why then did Moses command us to give a certificate of dismissal and to divorce her?" (v.7). His opponents clearly preferred to argue from Deuteronomy than from Genesis. Since there is no divorce legislation in the First Book of Moses, they wanted to parse the words of Book Five. Even so, they took liberties with their representation of the Mosaic legislation that Jesus was quick to challenge. Moses did not "command" (i.e., initiate, create, bless as part of God's plan) divorce but "allowed you to divorce your wives" because of your "hardhearted" behaviors (v.8). Although interpreters seem generally inclined to take the reference to hardheartedness as some sort of grudging consent to less-than-ideal behavior Jesus would eventually correct, the discussion of Deuteronomy 24:1-4 in Chapter Three of this book permits another equally plausible reading. Yahweh "allowed" divorce because of the unholy and "hardhearted" action of certain men in abusing their wives either by forcing them to remain tied to them in marriage (for only men could initiate divorce) or by jeopardizing their futures in allowing them to be reclaimed (if the spurned women somehow came into unexpected prosperity). On the second reading, divorce was not simply tolerated because times generally were evil and harsh in antiquity but because obdurate males were abusing their wives and children. It wasn't so much that hardhearted men wanted to divorce their wives as that they were so hardhearted toward women that they had been known to abuse, kill, or simply discard their wives as worthless property—and the Law of Moses "allowed" an alternative.

Having established his own higher ethical framework for it, Jesus returned to the original question that was put to him. What was his view of the circumstance(s) that might justify divorce? He repeated essentially the same stringently exaggerated statement he had made in the Sermon on the Mount: "And I say to you, whoever divorces his wife, except for unchastity, and marries another commits adultery" (v.9). Appealing yet again to information already given in this book, remember that *all* rabbinic interpreters would have agreed that only women could commit adultery. Men were allowed a degree of sexual latitude—not only in cases of polygamy but in the seriousness that would be attached to a sexual dalliance outside any legal arrangement—that women were never allowed. The possibility of a man's wife having a child by someone other than her husband and thus passing part or all of his estate to another family (i.e., bloodline) was so abhorrent that the Ancient Near East had a widespread and near-uniform policy of sexual exclusivity for married women that was not held to apply to male behavior. Jesus repudiated such casuistry and made it clear that males as well as females could violate the divine will and be judged guilty of adultery. In fact, he said, the only circumstance under which a man might put away his wife, remarry, and *not* be an adulterer would be for him to fall within the category of persons who had been faithful to their own marriage vows only to be the victim of sexual infidelity by his mate.

Upon hearing Jesus declare himself on the sacredness of marriage, some of his own disciples expressed a degree of dismay with his teaching. "If such is the case of a man with his wife, it is better not to marry," they said (v.10). In their world, marriage partners had far less idea about the temperament and personality traits of one another on their wedding day than those of us who choose our mates after a period of courtship. Arranged marriages and societies that looked with disdain on what we would call dating put one in a situation where marriage without the possibility of divorce was frightening to those good men. But Jesus did not retreat from the kingdom ideal he had just articulated. He said it would be spiritually preferable to embrace a eunuch's life (more hyperbole here!) than to ride the merry-go-round of divorce and remarriage that shows so little regard for God or community (vs.11-12). Indeed, as we will see in the chapters on Pauline literature, there were extreme circumstances of kingdom service that caused some Christians to forego marriage and thus become—in a metaphorical sense—"eunuchs for the sake of the kingdom of heaven."

Beth asked to talk with one of the elders of her church, and he agreed to meet her during Sunday School. Her daughter would be in class, and it would be a good time for them to visit. He asked permission to bring his wife to the meeting, and Beth agreed. The elder had no idea about the subject-matter of the meeting, and his wife wasn't sure she knew who Beth was. Was she upset over the recent resignation of the church's Youth Minister? Was something going on in her marriage?

As it turned out, something had been happening in Beth's marriage for several years. She had been incredibly busy with her career as a buyer for a chain of department stores. There had been lots of travel. And there had been a great deal of unhappiness brewing at home.

Her husband had served notice to Beth that he wanted a divorce. He would file for custody of their daughter, for he had been "Mr. Mom" in the house for the last years. He was tired of being married to an absentee spouse, and he wasn't going to continue it. He had told Beth he didn't love her anymore and that his decision was final. There would be no counseling. There would be no sessions with church leaders. There would be a divorce. And that was final.

If you had been in that room on that Sunday morning with Beth, what would you have said? What would you have done when the three of you left the room?

Mark 10:1-12

I have chosen to devote the major attention of this chapter to the words of Jesus in the Gospel of Matthew. But what about the parallels in Mark and Luke? There are issues of dating, dependency, and reasons for the abbreviated form in these Gospels that I must leave to the textual scholars.

Those technical matters do not affect the thesis I have developed in this chapter. I decided instead to explore the expanded and therefore more difficult texts in Matthew for two reasons. First, it is Matthew's account of the Savior's teaching on divorce and remarriage that is most often cited in discussions of the topic. Second, it is Matthew who introduces the "exception clause" and complicates the interpreter's task by making a distinction between the so-called guilty party and innocent party.[22]

For the sake of constructing a "redemptive theology" relative to divorce and remarriage, however, the Markan and Lukan texts may be easier and more direct than the Matthean material. They don't take us into the realm of deciding innocence and guilt. They do not explore exceptions. They both simply lay divorce at the feet of God for pardon.

> He left that place and went to the region of Judea and beyond the Jordan. And crowds again gathered around him; and, as was his custom, he again taught them.
>
> Some Pharisees came, and to test him they asked, "Is it lawful for a man to divorce his wife?" He answered them, "What did Moses command you?" They said, "Moses allowed a man to write a certificate of dismissal and to divorce her." But Jesus said to them, "Because of your hardness of heart he wrote this commandment for you. But from the beginning of creation, 'God made them male and female.' 'For this reason a man shall leave his father and mother and be joined to his wife, and the two shall become one flesh.' So they are no longer two, but one flesh. Therefore what God has joined together, let no one separate."
>
> Then in the house the disciples asked him again about this matter. He said to them, "Whoever divorces his wife and marries another commits adultery against her; and if she divorces her husband and marries another, she commits adultery."

Matthew and Mark both point out that this episode took place "beyond the Jordan." And this geographical note is probably very deliberate and important for our interpretation of it. This put Jesus in Perea, the territory of Herod Antipas. Antipas was the puppet ruler who had left his own wife, seduced his brother's wife (i.e., the infamous Herodias), and then married Herodias. He put John the Baptist to death for calling that sordid affair scandalous and wicked (cf. 6:14-29). Now that Jesus was in his territory, the question put to him may have been trying not only to alienate Jesus from some of his disciples along Hillelite-Shammaite lines of controversy but to trap him in the same snare that had been the Baptist's undoing. In both Gospels, it is clear that they weren't asking a serious question for the sake of information. They asked a question with an obvious context and—to use Mark's words—"tested him."

Rather than reply to them directly, Jesus answered their question with a question of his own. In the dialogue as related by Mark, the issue of commandment versus permission comes up. But the way the discussion proceeds is a bit different from Matthew's account. Again, I will leave those nuances to the textual scholars to sort out. "What did Moses command you?" Jesus asked. His well-versed questioners correctly replied, "Moses permitted a man to write a certificate of divorce and send her away." Moses didn't create divorce or bless it as a good thing. Because of what Jesus explained was the hardheartedness of people in spoiling their marriages and—in a male-dominated culture—men tossing out their wives, Yahweh had led Moses to affirm and protect women by having a "certificate of divorce" written for her before he could send her away.

In ancient cultures, there were no women's shelters and few ways for a divorced woman to live—honorably. Without her dowry and lacking an invitation to rejoin her family of origin, her options were limited. She could steal. Or she could prostitute herself. So the only honorable way for her to survive was to marry again as quickly as possible. But a mean-spirited former husband could make that difficult. He could refuse to confirm the divorce. If the woman proceeded to marry someone else, the first husband could treat her as his "property," reclaim her from the new husband, and make her life miserable. But Deuteronomy 24:1-4 gives her an important protection. If a Jewish man henceforth chose to divorce his wife, he had to give her a written certificate of divorce. When she remarried, he could make no further claim against her person or her property. For him to do so would be "abhorrent to the Lord."

All this information repeated yet again in summary form basically means that Jesus' words in this text are descriptive rather than prescriptive. That is, he was not giving a new law on divorce and remarriage to replace the one Moses had articulated. The moral laws of the Old and New Testaments are continuous and identical, for they grow from and reflect the intrinsic holiness of God. And God's nature had not changed from Moses' time to that of Jesus. He was not lax on divorce and remarriage in the Old Testament, only to get tough in the New. He is just as concessive now as he was then; he was just as restrictive then as he is now.

So what Jesus said that day is that Antipas and Herodias had defied God's will about the sanctity of marriage. They had committed adultery. He wasn't about to back away from John's preaching that had affirmed the Law of Moses. When Jesus got alone in the house with his disciples, they asked him to spell out the implications of what he had told the Pharisees. So he said, "Anyone who divorces his wife and marries another woman commits adultery against her. And if she divorces her husband and marries another man, she commits adultery."

When you think about it, Jesus said nothing novel here. He simply looked into the faces of both his would-be tormenters and his inquisitive disciples and said, "When somebody—whether great or small—does the sort of thing Herod and Herodias have just done, they stand convicted before the Law of faithlessness, covenant-breaking, adultery. Moses told you that long, long ago. Neither Herod nor one of you has the right to be faithless toward your wives." *Case closed*. Again, this is not new law. It is the reading and application of the Law of Moses.

Now please notice something that people typically miss in Mark's account of this episode: "Whoever divorces his wife and marries another commits adultery against her." Did you catch it? "Adultery" is what a man does "against" his first wife if he tosses her aside for someone else. Has anyone ever told you that divorce may sometimes be a "necessary evil" to protect a woman or her children from abuse, alcoholism, or other terrible situation but that her remarriage would be adultery? That is *not* what Jesus said!

Tim and Bob were both on their high school basketball team. Tim was the power forward, and Bob was the shooting guard. They didn't just play basketball together but were friends. Their class schedules were almost identical for four years. They even dated twin sisters who were a year behind them in school.

For all they had in common, Tim and Bob were very different. Tim was from a devout Christian home, and Bob's parents neither attended church nor saw to the spiritual education of their three sons. The two best friends talked some about God and the Bible, but the conversations just never went that far. They could talk more easily about basketball, school, and their girlfriends.

Tim was disappointed but not shocked when Bob confided that he and his girlfriend were sleeping together. "Don't you wish you weren't so 'hung up on religion'?" he chided his friend. "You could be having some fun too!" Tim thought it might be a test—a test of his Christian character. If he could show Bob that he could keep his standards, respect his girlfriend, and maintain his own purity, it just might have a positive effect on Bob.

Now fast-forward eleven years. Tim and Bob graduated from high school. They went to different colleges. And they lost contact with each other—except for occasional times in their hometown at holidays. The ten-year class reunion was on the horizon. Both planned to be there.

Tim and Bob were thrilled to be together. They ate together. Tim was with the twin sister he had married just after graduation, and Bob was with a woman he introduced to them for the first time.

The two men were the subject-matter for several stories others told from their memories of high school. When the evening came to an end, they weren't through talking. Bob in particular said he wanted some private time. The women insisted they understood, and Bob's date said she would drive Tim's wife home. So the guys went to a coffee shop and began to talk.

"Tim, I want to apologize to you for the grief I gave you about God and faith and church back when we were so close. How I wish I had listened to you back then! I could have found Christ so much sooner!

"You see, what I started in high school only picked up speed at State Tech. I was a party animal. I soon broke up with my half of our twin sisters! But I found lots more. And I slept with more of them than I can recall. I was a real jerk back then.

"But something happened about eight months ago. I am saved now, and my life is different. I met a woman who is 'the love of my life'—the woman who was with us at the class reunion tonight. Suzanne loves Jesus more than me, and the thing that makes me so sure that I want to marry her is her faith. I am so ashamed of all the partying and one-night stands. But I have repented of all that, and Christ has forgiven it! Thank God! Now Suzanne and I are going to get married next summer, and I want you to be my best man."

An astonished former teammate toyed with his coffee cup, as he tried to figure out where to begin. He wasn't even sure he could speak. But he collected himself.

"Bob, I'm thrilled to hear what you have just shared with me. I think I always knew your heart. And I always believed you would wind up following Jesus. It would just take the right person and the right timing for you to hear his call. Suzanne seems like a wonderful lady, and I can understand why she got your attention.

"I just wish things were that good for Ellen and me. She was at the reunion tonight just to 'humor me' and so she could see some of the people we haven't seen in a long time. But I'll bet you felt the cold between us. Our divorce will be final in 17 days.

"You see, I cheated on her several months ago. It was a short-lived thing with a woman who doesn't mean anything to me. But Ellen found out. I made it worse by lying about it at first! By the time I admitted what she knew, it was too late. I had dealt the fatal blow to our marriage.

"From what I've always heard at my church, you have every right to marry Suzanne. You slept with how many—a dozen, 50, 100 women? But you were smart enough not to marry one of them. Now that you have turned your life over to God, you are forgiven and can start fresh. You can get married and be *happy. But I was 'the good boy' who waited and 'made an honest woman' of Ellen—only to throw it all away with one affair. She'll divorce me, move on with her life, and I will never be able to get married with God's blessing."*

There was a long silence. Bob broke it with this: "Tim, I'm new at this religious stuff and sure don't claim to be a Bible scholar. But that just doesn't make any sense! Because I slept around instead of getting married, I'm 'in the clear'? And you tried to do right by getting married to Ellen—only to mess up once and, what, have to become a monk to go to heaven?"

Are grace and hope only for those who come to Christ at the end of a long period of moral irresponsibility? Do they also apply to those who break faith after a long period of spiritual fidelity in marriage? Does repentance mean more in one case than in the other? Does the blood of Christ cover more in one case than in the other?

In Mark's account, divorce and remarriage are treated in even more direct and austere language than in Matthew. Exceptional cases are not in view. Divorce—whether remarriage ever occurs or not—is adultery (i.e., covenant-breaking, faithlessness). Both Old and New Testaments assume that divorced people will remarry, and there is no prohibition against doing so. Yet those second marriages are not immoral situations where a man and woman are "living in adultery." People may adulterate, breach, or otherwise abuse their marriage covenants by breaking a one-flesh union. That said, they are not "living in sin" if they marry again. And their effective repentance from the adultery they committed by ending a marriage without justification plays out in making the new marriage work.

There is no biblical precedent for telling someone to leave a second (or later) marriage in order to set things right with God relative to a previous marital failure. In fact, we should always remember that reclaiming one's former mate is the one thing specifically forbidden in Deuteronomy 24:1-4. If you are in a second, third, or fourth marriage today, the call of God to you has nothing to do with getting out of your present relationship and trying to get back with your first mate. It has everything to do with making your present relationship as healthy and divorce-proof as possible.

Suppose, for example, that John and Mary are decent Christian people who—maybe for the sake of their children when they had no other motivation—have tried to make their marriage work. They spent years and thousands of dollars on counseling. It was all done in good faith. But it wasn't working and wasn't going to work. So they get a divorce—and are told they can never marry again (for neither was sexually unfaithful to the marriage) and never function in a leadership role in the church again. Oh, by the way, they are warned that they will both be excommunicated from the church if they do marry again. Or perhaps it is only the first to marry again who will be excluded from the church's fellowship. And then a legalistic mindset would allow someone to declare the person who can wait longer to remarry an "innocent party" and bless his or her marriage. What a horrible mockery of righteousness, grace, and redemption. No wonder unbelievers sometimes look in on the actions of the church only to cringe—and further justify their antipathy toward all things religious.

Luke 16:18

Finally, there is the statement of Jesus about divorce and remarriage in the Gospel of Luke. It "pops up" with minimal context and has none of the interpretive keys provided either by Matthew or Mark for the texts we have just studied. But as we become less inclined to embrace Pharisaic legalism and begin to exhibit kingdom hearts, who is to say this is not the single most helpful statement from Jesus to our situation? Jesus said, "Anyone who divorces his wife and marries another commits adultery, and whoever marries a woman divorced from her husband commits adultery."

Why is this text potentially the most helpful of all? It is the most direct and unequivocal statement from Jesus to the effect that divorce is not a good thing, not part of the ideal will of God, and not anything to be happy about. It is, in fact, something more often than not to be repented of—repented of in the confidence that God is in the business of forgiving sin and healing sinners.

I have already pointed out several times that the essential feature of adultery is not sex but covenant-breaking. Adultery is worse than fornication under Old Testament statutes for the simple reason that fornication, though wrong, does not involve the element of personal betrayal that adultery entails. And, as the statement stands in Luke, it is difficult to say that anybody involved—whether male or female, divorcer or divorced, terminator of a first marriage or contractor of a second with a divorcee— is "in the clear." When a marriage fails, my own experience as a bystander, counselor, or friend says that everybody is likely to suffer. Luke's account of the teaching of Jesus on divorce and remarriage seems to acknowledge just that. But if that is so, will redemption and recovery from it not be along the lines of all redemption and recovery effected by the Son of God?

In summary, I believe the teaching of Jesus on divorce and remarriage includes the following important elements:

First, Jesus affirmed and upheld what the Law of Moses says on divorce and remarriage. That is, he did not come to give "new laws" on the subject but to show us that righteousness always requires more than law. Laws are necessary to righteousness but they are not sufficient for it to be realized. Hearts must be transformed by renewal that can come only from above, and transformation must show itself in how people who claim to love God live out the implications of their love for one another. This is the righteousness that both "exceeds that of the scribes and Pharisees" and allows one to "enter the kingdom of heaven."

Second, Jesus acknowledged that divorce is a part of human experience. It does not exist in human experience because of God's will but on account of our own human weakness, sinfulness, and hardness of heart.

Third, Jesus reflected on the fact that law was designed to protect some of the most vulnerable victims of divorce. Women (and their children) were intended to have special protection against exploitation in the community of Israel. Again, however, human sinfulness allowed some within the community to evade the point of those protections and to perpetuate and even to expand harm to women in a male-dominated culture.

Fourth, divorce is a failure to experience God's desire for human marital relationships. It exposes human sinfulness in dramatic fashion. It is not the divorce decree—which is nothing more than the legal acknowledgement of the death of a relationship—but whatever the man or woman has done to put the relationship to death that is sinful.

Fifth, the person who seeks and initiates a divorce—especially one who involves a third party in sexual infidelity—is guilty of "adultery against" his or her mate in the most flagrant way. In fact, the harm "against" others seems almost never to end in such cases. Eventually, every life touched by any of the parties involved is likely to be hurt and wounded by what happens. Families of origin, children to the once-married pair, future mates—all will pay a price of some sort for the dissolution of a marital union.

Sixth, adultery is not an unpardonable sin. Can we really believe—regardless of the heartache, damaged lives, and lifelong consequences that are involved—that a sinner whose offense is divorce (i.e., covenant-breaking, adultery) has no spiritual option but to live with his or her brokenness forever? Do the Gospels reveal a Jesus who can heal blind eyes, forgive his own murderers, and let drug traffickers have a full range of life options for the future but cannot (or will not) heal the broken life of someone who fails at marriage? Repentance is one's genuine remorse over whatever he or she contributed to the breakup of a marriage, and forgiveness is always the divine response to a penitent heart.

Seventh, repentance and forgiveness entail the possibility of healing, moving ahead with life, and experiencing the good things one had otherwise forfeited. In the case of divorcees, this means that remarriage is an option to consider. For some, though, getting married again may be inappropriate. One may have discovered that he or she is not capable of sustaining the intimacy of marriage. Indeed, there may be other factors about personality, lifestyle, or career that would make it advisable for him or her to remain single following a divorce.

Eighth, remaining single following divorce is neither a penance nor a penalty upon which forgiveness is contingent. Divorced persons have the option of experiencing God's gracious pardon, learning from the mistakes of a failed marriage, and receiving his final touch of spiritual healing through a new marital relationship. The message of the New Testament about every human failure is grace, pardon, and healing. Divorce is not a sin in its own special class that requires a lifelong penance of remaining single, celibate, and companionless.

She and her husband had been married four years when Janise went to the church's counseling center. "Something must be wrong with me!" she began— trying to hold back tears that soon came anyway. "I don't know what it will take to make him happy, but I can't connect with Kevin anymore."

The experienced female counselor she had chosen to see was gentle but persistent in trying to get specifics that would help her make sense of Janise's frustration. As she went deeper into the relationship of a pained young woman and her husband, she learned that there had been no sexual intimacy in the marriage for three years and seven months.

"Do you think your husband will come for counseling too?" she asked Janise. She was a bit surprised when Janise told her that Kevin had suggested that she should go to a counselor and that he would be willing to participate too.

After two joint sessions, the counselor sensed a need for talking with Kevin alone. What she suspected turned out to be true.

Kevin had lived with his homosexual partner during college. When they graduated and went separate ways, Kevin tried to "go straight" for the sake of what he had been taught from the Bible. It had been a miserable failure, and now he had ruined Janise's life! He told the counselor he had considered suicide.

No, he had not seen his former lover. No, he had not begun a new relationship with someone else. He knew that would be wrong, and he wasn't going to sell his soul for sex with a gay partner. He could live alone. He could be a "eunuch for the kingdom." But he could not lie to Janise—or to himself— any longer.

"I want her to forget about me and get on with her life," he said of Janise. "I really do 'love' her, but I can't 'make love to' her. And she deserves somebody who will make her feel special."

Then came a question the counselor had never been asked before. "Do I need to go out and have sex with a guy for Janise's sake? Or can she divorce me and be okay with the church?"

As they talked further, Kevin explained that he had been studying and knew the Bible permitted divorce for sexual sin. Was his lack of interest in Janise sufficient grounds for her to divorce him and marry somebody else down the way? Or did he need to have sex with somebody to set her free?

The counselor had never been in such a predicament before. Someone was asking her advice about doing something he knew was wrong—in order to keep someone else from doing something many in their church would say was wrong.

Ninth, marriages subsequent to a divorce are real marriages. That is, anyone who has divorced and remarried is actually married to the new mate—not "living in adultery" with that person or "still married to her first husband in the eyes of God." A civil divorce terminates a marriage. And anyone with a legal divorce has both the civil and divine right to marry again. In the Gospels, after all, Jesus talked with and saved a woman who had been married to five different men and, at the time she met the Messiah, was living with a man she had not bothered to marry (John 4:16-18). Her life was out of control; her solution was not to somehow reconnect with her first husband but to allow Jesus to transform her and make her new.

Tenth, there is no biblical precedent for breaking up a second (or later!) marriage in order to set right the mistakes made in the first. While Jesus made it clear that some marriages are broken without justification, he did not tell us how to "fix" them. Again, while saying that people who take marriage so lightly as to put away their wives in order to marry another are guilty of adultery by doing so, he did not specify what should happen to those new marriages. We must not presume to impose solutions that do not come from a clear word from Jesus on the matter.

By the power of the Holy Spirit, chastity and holiness are gifts to the children of God. By the presence of Christ in a marriage, two people not only become one flesh but are made holy to God. What law could never accomplish, the presence and power of God make real. Adultery becomes unthinkable—not because of law and one's fear of sin, judgment, and hell but—because renewed hearts seek and live renewed lives. They form wholesome relationships. They learn to love one another as they have been loved by God.

By grace, people who have failed at marriage and who have divorced for the worst or most trivial of reasons may be redeemed from guilt. People who have destroyed marriages through their adulteries can be pardoned. People whose hearts and behaviors have been cold, hard, and unfeeling can be made whole. And this is by forgiveness and renewal from above—not through another divorce, not by the penance of celibacy, and not by unringing the bell of harm already done. What law cannot do, grace accomplishes. What law cannot undo, Christ's blood forgives. What our legalistic interpretations have confused, the redemptive presence of the Holy Spirit can sanctify.

Thank God for a righteousness that exceeds, surpasses, and triumphs over that of the Pharisees and scribes—both ancient and modern.

CHAPTER SIX

PAUL ON DIVORCE AND REMARRIAGE
PART 1

Paul had to face the same predicament we encounter in taking the words of Jesus and applying them redemptively to the life
situations of people for whom he cared deeply. Fortunately for
us, he had the special empowerment of the Spirit of God to
guide him. The Apostle to the Gentiles took the words he had
learned in a Jewish context and used them to answer a variety
of questions we still face. We should study not only his answers
but his general method of applying Scripture to hard questions
on this subject.

The place where everything found in Scripture about marriage,
divorce, and remarriage comes together for present-day believers is in
the writings of Paul to the church at Corinth. At least, that is what happened in my case. Having been taught to apply the hyperbolic statements
of Jesus in the Gospels with wooden literalism to relationships in disarray,
I finally stumbled across Paul—only to marvel at his previous exclusion
from my studies of divorce and remarriage. Although we typically think
and speak of Paul as an apostle and evangelist, he was also a pastoral presence among the churches he planted and for persons to whom he had
taught the gospel. His epistles contain not only explications of the gospel

but also apply the message of Christ to particular situations of church life and personal Christian faith. His method is less to lay out general principles for the Christians to apply as to address particular cases from which we are left to draw more comprehensive insights.

There is not a case study in the Pauline Epistles to parallel every situation we face today. Indeed, there is so much about every human life and marital situation that is unique that such a document could never be written. There would always be the novel situation for which there is no specific parallel. Again, however, the very desire for such a book likely betrays our fondness for legalism in reading Holy Scripture. As explained earlier in this volume, it is our penchant for treating the Bible principally as a collection of legal documents that has generated many of the heartaches we have created with the interpretation of the Word of God relative to broken lives.

In 1 Corinthians, Paul addresses a number of questions that had been put to him about celibacy, marriage, the disruption of marriages by death and divorce, and remarriage following death or divorce. What he says to these questions is invaluable for our instruction. He deals with a limited number of specific situations, yet he deals with enough to provide some parameters that can be most helpful to us.

In the first place, it is important to remember that Paul is especially qualified to teach us on this topic. He was Jewish by birth, steeped in the rabbinic study of Torah, and clearly aware—as will be demonstrated directly—of what Jesus had said about divorce in the Law of Moses. Yet he was also aware of Roman culture and law, for he had grown up in the free city of Tarsus and was himself a Roman citizen. The dual circumstance of being rooted in Holy Scripture and struggling to honor its demand of holiness in a pagan culture put him precisely where we are. We know the Bible teaches a high view of marriage and family stability, yet we also live in a culture where marital commitments are taken far too lightly and divorces are granted far too frequently.

Second, Paul becomes our teacher here as a Christian ethicist in modeling how the teachings of Jesus on divorce should be applied. The goal he keeps before his readers is always reconciliation in the current relationship rather than rushing into a new one. In this regard, he is both very Jesus-like and very pastoral; whatever has led to the failure of one relationship may well lead to the failure of another, so it is preferable to resolve problems rather than merely flee from them and create another similar situation. (Likely all of us have seen it happen. Someone changes job, mate, residence, and church—but remains troubled, unhappy, and angry. One gets the impression he is dragging his problems with him, no matter the new context in which they surface.) Paul is also very realistic in acknowledging that the ideal will not always be achieved, and some people will pursue divorce in spite of Jesus' words and the apostle's counsel based on them.

In the third place, one should notice that Paul does not try to give a set of inflexible rules for solving complex dilemmas in human relationships. He appeals to each believer's desire to honor Christ in a culture that is often hostile to faith. He clearly expects that desire to be extended to one's behavior toward a mate (or potential mate), one's larger family-by-blood, and his or her still larger family-by-faith.

Mitchell and Amy married just out of high school. Mitchell's parents offered to pay his tuition through college, and he eventually completed an M.B.A. Amy worked at a plant in the city where Mitchell was enrolled in school and earned their living expenses. Both were Christians and sincerely committed to each other. School and work were demanding, but they had no more problems during the first few years of marriage than most couples face.

Mitchell settled into his career, and Amy quit work to begin their family. They had two children in three years. The growing family moved twice, each time to a larger and nicer house. They appeared to be doing well.

Then something started happening with Mitchell. During a recessionary period, his company was hit particularly hard. He worked day and night to keep things afloat. Amy hardly saw him at all. It was just as well, for, when he was at home, life was unpleasant for her and the children. The stress had gotten to him, and Mitchell was always tense and grumpy. His outbursts of temper often made the children cry.

Once when Amy confronted him in tears about what he was doing to their family and asked him to talk with their minister or a marriage counselor, he cursed her and became violent. He broke a lamp and put a bruise on Amy's arm where he squeezed her so tightly. His tirades became more frequent and more dangerous. When he exploded one night and threw their son's baseball glove at him, Amy had taken all she could.

Amy went to an attorney. Mitchell was forced to move to an apartment, and she and the children stayed in the family's house. It was apparent that the new arrangement suited Mitchell just fine. He seldom called, made only a few child-support payments during their separation, and used less than a third of his visitation times with the children.

Amy went back to work at a kindergarten and kept pleading with Mitchell to see a marriage counselor with her. He swore he would never do so and didn't care if he never saw her again. He filed for divorce, and it became final in the fall of last year.

During the spring semester at her school, Amy became friends with the assistant principal. Brian had never married and was two years older than Amy. They talked occasionally and went to dinner once.

One of Amy's friends from church came to her and insisted the friendship with Brian had to stop. "Mitchell treated you terribly," she said, "but you know he was never unfaithful to you. If you fall in love with and marry Brian, you'll be living in adultery. Then Mitchell will be the 'innocent party' and free to get married without fault. You might even be put out of our church. Just be patient, Amy. I hear that Mitchell has started drinking. It won't be long until he gets lonely and wants to be with a woman. He'll break. Then you'll be free to marry Brian."

Would you give this counsel? Does it sound like something you would expect Jesus to say? If you had been in the conversation, what counsel would you have given?

Through the first six chapters of 1 Corinthians, Paul has done two significant things. In chapters 1-4, he has challenged a divided church to regroup in unity around the central message of the cross. It was not the preachers who delivered the message but the Christ on whom the message centers who deserved their loyalty. Then, in chapters 5-6, he has called for a united church to live in a way that would be appropriate to their identity as the body of Christ. As an island of holiness in the Corinthian culture, they were encouraged not to tolerate brazenly immoral behavior in their midst. If necessary, they were to excommunicate a member who defied the demand of holiness. The church must not only be different from the worst in its environment but must even make judgments against its own who would bring the world's pollutions into the church. While any form of persistent wrongdoing could justify such a radical reaction, the Christians at Corinth were warned against sexual immorality (Gk, *porneia*) in particular.

Beginning with chapter 7, Paul turns from the flow of his argument about unity in the gospel, holiness before the world, and sexual purity to address some questions that had been put to him in writing. First Corinthians thus has the distinction of being an epistle in response to an epistle. We could wish we had the questions in their original form to help us with the interpretation of Paul's answers to them. "Now concerning the matters about which you wrote . . ." opens the section of the epistle where he steadily works through the list of situations about which he had received inquiry from Corinth (7:25; 8:1; 12:1; 16:1, 12).

Issues Involving Believers (1 Cor 7:1-11)

The first eleven verses address various marital situations where all parties involved are Christians. Instead of basing the things he will say on the words of Christ we have studied in the previous two chapters, Paul works toward the Savior's statement of the divine ideal for marriage and waits to quote him at v.10. He opens instead with a statement that ties back to the exhortation he had just given about sexual purity and the Christian duty of abstaining from all forms of unchaste behavior. Because of the cultural setting of a seaport town filled not only with brothels for visiting sailors but idolatrous pagan cults that gloried in sexual license, the apostle was compelled to give clear and direct instruction about what constituted proper sexual conduct for people who had committed themselves to follow Christ.

Some of the Corinthian disciples appear to have taken the Christian rejection of *porneia* to mean that celibacy was a morally superior lifestyle. They appear to have developed a slogan to summarize their point of view: "It is well for a man not to touch a woman" (v.1). Paul's response was to say that marriage is the better response to sexual temptation than some widespread attempt at urging abstinence from sex. "Because of cases of sexual immorality (*porneia*), each man should have his own wife and each woman her own husband" (v.2). In a rather remarkable section, he insists that not only do men have authority over the bodies of their wives for sexual intimacies but so also do women have equal authority over the bodies of their husbands. Thus a husband and wife must be considerate of the other with regard to conjugal rights, and they should only rarely—and then only by mutual consent—enter extended periods of sexual abstinence; otherwise, Satan might be able to entice them into sin by testing the limits of their self-control (vs.3-5). Even so, abstinence by married couples is never a "command" and certainly was not a means to moral superiority—as some were contending at Corinth; at best, it was only a "concession" to special circumstances (v.6). Far from a command to all, the celibate life is a gift (Gk, *charisma*) to the few such as Paul (v.7).[23]

For our study of divorce and remarriage, there are certainly those who believe that a celibate life is the only option open to persons who have been divorced for their infidelity to an innocent party or who have ended their marriages for such reasons as incompatibility, mental cruelty, or failure to be a responsible parent. One is forced to wonder if those who interpret Scripture so as to bind such a penalty believe God gives the gift of celibacy to all who pursue such divorces. If not, the conclusion would seem to be that celibacy for the rest of one's life is either a punishment for being divorced or a penance required for forgiveness. To the contrary, Paul takes up the matter of divorcees and their fate in order to give them explicit permission to remarry following divorce—a permission that some (perhaps the celibacy advocates) appear to have denied them.

To the unmarried and the widows I say that it is well for them to remain unmarried as I am. But if they are not practicing self-control, they should marry. For it is better to marry than to be aflame with passion.

To the married I give this command—not I but the Lord—that the wife should not separate from her husband (but if she does separate, let her remain unmarried or else be reconciled to her husband), and that the husband should not divorce his wife. (7:8-11)

The word "unmarried" in 8a and 11a is translated from the Greek term *agamos*.[24] It is formed by adding an alpha-prefix (i.e., as with our English "un-," "in-," or "a-" in words such as unyielding, inhospitable, or atheistic) to the word for marriage. Someone who is *agamos* is either someone who has never married or who once was married but now is not. The term is therefore broad enough to include single, widowed, and divorced persons. It should be understood to embrace all these categories, unless the context clearly restricts its meaning.

For the study of Pauline teaching on divorce and remarriage, it is important to realize that this encompassing term always includes divorcees. Since Paul has specific terms for a widowed person (*chera*, v.8) or the never-married person (*parthenos*, vs.25,28,34,36, 37,38), *agamos* is best understood here as referring principally to divorced persons (cf. vs.8,11,32,34) and to widows and never-married persons by logical extension. That this is true seems undeniable from verse 11, where *agamos* is the word used of a woman who had separated from (*chorizo* = divorce) her husband.

Paul also uses the term *agamos* (vv. 8,11,32) meaning the "unmarried," as distinct from widows (v. 8). This includes those who have never been married and those who have been married and are now unmarried. This can be seen from Paul's use of *agamos* in v. 11, where "unmarried" is used of the wife who has separated from her husband. What Paul proceeds to say applies equally to the single, widowers and widows and the divorced. But the particular argument is drawn from the case of the divorced, and applies *a fortiori* to the others. He begins by saying that his observations are not based upon a specific command of the Lord. He concludes by saying that it is not a sin for anyone in their position to marry.[25]

If one were to argue that *agamos* does not include divorcees, he is forced to make the improbable claim that Paul wrote 40 verses on marriage problems to a church in a notoriously decadent city and never felt the need to speak about the situation of divorced men and women. That would seem highly unlikely. To the contrary, these notoriously complex situations would surely be among those most troubling to a church trying to find its way to a clear path for modeling the gospel in a wide-open city. In three references to divorcees, the Apostle to the Gentiles treats three different situations. In the first instance (vs.8-9), he counsels those already divorced to remain single.[26] He does not require it, however, in view of the larger issue of sexual immorality. For those without the gift of celibacy, he not only permits but encourages remarriage. "For it is better to marry than to be aflame with passion." In the second case (vs.10-11), where a believer was still married to another Christian but sensed significant jeopardy in that relationship, he echoed the words of Jesus. Neither husband nor wife was supposed to separate from the other; if either should do so, the obligation at that point was not to seek a new mate but to explore the possibilities for reconciliation.

Paul's guidance represents not only good theology but good pastoral counsel. A Christian whose marriage is in trouble should be reminded of the no-divorce ideal taught in Scripture and affirmed by Jesus. But Paul was also a realist who knew that some marriages do break down and result in the separation[27] of partners. He counseled against a move by either one of them to establish a new marriage, and he was not secretive about his motive for doing so. He hoped that a time of cooling off, conversation, intervention by concerned parties, and moderation of positions might lead to reconciliation. There is still a third case involving divorcees that will emerge later in the chapter at verses 27-28. This third case specifically addresses anyone who might hear "but if she does separate, let her remain unmarried or else be reconciled to her husband" as a prohibition of remarriage, and it will be dealt with when we reach that section of text in Chapter Seven of this volume.

Issues Involving Unbelievers (1 Cor 7:12-16)

Having offered pastoral guidance to Christians who were considering divorce or who had already separated, Paul turns his attention "to the rest" of the Corinthian believers who were married—those whose mates were non-Christians. One should not read his comment "I say—I and not the Lord" as a disclaimer of confidence about his counsel but as an affirmation of his apostolic authority to give it. Toward the end of the epistle, he will say this: "Anyone who claims to be a prophet, or to have spiritual powers, must acknowledge that what I am writing to you is a command of the Lord" (14:37; cf. 7:40b). He had responded to the believer-believer marriage plight by quoting well-known words from Jesus.[28] Now, by the authority he had been given from the Holy Spirit, he extended them to believer-unbeliever relationships as well. That extension would have a significant caveat.

The essence of Paul's instruction to any Christian whose mate was still an unbeliever was that he or she should continue in the marriage *if possible*. But continuing the relationship was nothing Paul could mandate to a non-Christian, of course, and would depend altogether on whether the person "consents" to stay with his or her Christian mate (vs.12-13). In other words, Paul is realistic about the prospects for saving such marriages. The Christian mate was now obliged to put the Kingdom of God above all else, and that very determination would not be well-received by a husband or wife who was hostile to the new faith that had come to Corinth via Paul's evangelistic ministry. In situations where Christians could remain in their mixed marriages, they had the potential to "make holy" (NRSV) or "sanctify" (NIV) the other adult and any children in the family (v.14). These words do not mean, of course, that the saving faith of Christians would somehow transfer redeeming merit to other family members. The Greek word translated "make holy" or "sanctify" (*hagiazo* = set apart, dedicate) is best understood here to say that the best hope for reaching non-Christian mates or children is through the faithful exhibition of Christ-presence in that home by a believer. Thus verse 16: "Wife, for all you know, you might save your husband. Husband, for all you know, you might save your wife." By logical extension, the same thing was to be assumed by fathers and mothers about their unbelieving children.

There was always the obvious possibility that a non-Christian mate would *not* consent to stay married to the husband or wife whose first allegiance had become Jesus of Nazareth. What then? "But if the unbelieving partner separates, let it be so; in such a case the brother or sister is not bound. It is to peace that God has called you" (v.15). Consistent with the Christian ethical principle stressed by Jesus in the Sermon on the Mount and underscored by Paul in Romans 12, the ideal would be to have harmony within a family. Reject divorce. Seek reconciliation. For the sake of all parties involved, continue to live together peacefully. When the ideal is not within reach, however, divorce may be the only path to peace. While doing everything reasonably possible to bring about reconciliation, church leaders must be careful not to create an impossible burden of guilt for a man or woman who chooses divorce. Yes, some may resort to divorce too quickly and with too little regard for the negative consequences that could come. But most of us have known people who have not only "lost the best years of their lives" but their chance at what the Bible elsewhere calls "a quiet and peaceable life in all godliness and dignity" (2 Tim 2:2b) by staying in hopeless marriages.

Rob and Helen married the summer after they graduated from college, and the preacher had never met Rob when Helen showed up at his office the first time. She was crying when she came in with her infant in her arms, and he asked if she would mind if his assistant sat in on their meeting. Helen looked up, darted her eyes at the woman, and nodded. What did it matter? She didn't know either the preacher or his assistant. And she would need help with her little girl who was awake and stirring.

The preacher suggested they begin with prayer. He heard Helen sobbing quietly through his words to God—asking for his presence, for Helen's sense of security in talking with him, and for guidance in knowing how to respond.

Helen gave a bit of her history—background in a religious family, graduation from the local college, and marriage to a man she truly loved. No, he was not a Christian. No, he never attended church with her. But he had never tried to stop her from being part of the church. The issue was Leslie.

Leslie was three and a half months old. Her birth had been such a wonderful event for Helen and Rob, for they had tried to have a baby for nearly three years before Leslie was conceived. But now the presence of their baby girl was threatening their marriage.

As Helen got ready for church last Sunday, Rob had informed her in no uncertain terms that Leslie wasn't going with her. "I can take care of her for an hour," he said. "She's just been fed. I know how to rock and change diapers."

"But I told some people Leslie would be out for the first time today and they could see her!"

"They'll never see her down there at your church!" Rob fired back. "I know enough about churches to know that a child of mine will never set foot in the place! They're not safe for kids. And my kid isn't going to be hurt like I was."

Rob had told Helen shortly before they married that something happened to him at a church camp when he was 11 that had kept him from church ever since. They didn't pursue it. She just knew she loved him—and believed things would change after their wedding. Although he had never told Helen she couldn't go to church, it was clear that things were going to be different with Leslie. He was adamant. And he said there was no way he would ever change his mind.

The preacher quizzed Helen about how she thought Rob would respond to his request to talk. Maybe he could be reasoned with about all this. She wasn't sure. And she asked, "What if he just won't relent? What if he says my baby can't be with me? Does he have the right to say she can't learn about Jesus? Do I have to submit to him on something that important?"

What would you have done in the preacher's situation? In Helen's? What if nothing has changed six months or a year after this first conversation? Then what would you advise Helen to do?

A General Principle: Peace (1 Cor 7:17-24)

The next eight verses have nothing directly to do with marriage, divorce, and remarriage. They constitute a parenthetical comment on the reconciliation-peace principle Paul had applied to marriage at v.15. Whereas some commentaries call these verses a "digression," it is better to see them as a bridge between the reconciliation-peace principle he has just applied to mixed marriages and the counsel he will give to all Christians in dealing with marital conundrums generally.

Consistent with Paul's view of Jew-Greek, slave-free, and male-female equality in Christ (cf. Gal 3:28), he urged Christians to use their freedom and equality in ways that were not needlessly disruptive. Was one of the several false charges against Christianity that it encouraged sedition and social unrest? Did some charge that Christian freedom was a cloak for shameless behaviors? It was not true! Christians were consistently taught to obey the authorities and to honor the law (Rom 13:1ff). Many Christians were from the slave classes, yet they were ordered to be more compliant and productive in their new lives—as a positive testimony to Christ (Eph 6:5-8). Christian wives were instructed to be particularly submissive to the authority of their husbands, lest their behavior as part of Christ's "new creation" be misunderstood and become a barrier to their husbands' faith (Eph 5:22ff; cf. 1 Pet 3:1ff).

As a general principle, then, the fact that God has called Christians to peace seems to mean that we should regard the *status quo* at the time of our conversion to be "the life that the Lord has assigned" us to live (v.17). That is, receiving Christ's freedom from sin and death was not to be interpreted as the right to be disruptive. "Let each of you remain in the condition in which you were called" (v.20).

But is this—as I called it in the paragraph above—a "general principle" of Christian conduct or a "biblical law for Christian behavior"? It is clearly the former, in spite of the tendency of people such as me to read every imperative of Scripture as an inflexible rule or a legal stipulation. How can we be sure? Against the general principle of Jews not seeking "to remove the marks of circumcision" and telling Greeks they should "not seek circumcision" (vs.18-19), Paul would later have Timothy circumcised for the sake of including him in his missionary work among Jewish people (Acts 16:1-5). In spite of the maxim about staying in the condition in which one was called, he reasoned in this immediate context that a slave able to secure his or her freedom could "make use of your present [liberated] condition now more than ever" (vs.21-23).

Paul is treading the thin ice Christian pastors, teachers, and friends always must tread when dealing with persons whose marriages are in serious trouble. "My situation is unbearable!" the person insists. "Does my Christian commitment require me to remain in this awful situation?" Against the opinion of many, there is not a law to answer this heart-wrenching question. There are principles to weigh in trying to make a prayerful, responsible choice.

The law-answers-all mindset might look at the Helen and Rob case presented earlier and give a quick, definitive answer. "If Rob has not been sexually unfaithful to Helen, she cannot divorce him and marry somebody else," comes the authoritarian reply. "If she does divorce him because of his mistreatment of their daughter in forbidding her to learn about Jesus, I can understand that. But she can't marry again. If she does, she will be living in adultery." I understand the thought process that generates that answer. It is the one I would have offered in good faith 30 years ago, for I had been taught to read and apply every imperative statement of Scripture as an unbending rule for Christian conduct.

Can you not imagine that women in the first century were sometimes put in this situation of choosing between husband and Christ? Women had very little independence in those days, and they would have had no legal recourse to challenge her husbands. Women are still put in those situations. It is more likely to happen, as it did in Helen's case, over the freedom to take a child to church, teach the child of Jesus, and pass her faith to her offspring.

Rob and Helen's case is real and has a wide range of ever-so-slight variations. How are we to be guided by Scripture in dealing with these situations? Should a child be put in a situation where it is impossible for her to know the gospel? Does God expect a mother or father to put a child in such spiritual jeopardy? If the child deserves to be protected by the parent, does God penalize the parent for doing so? There are far more principles than rules in Scripture, and the rules are to be read and applied on the basis of the overarching principles that justify them. Both principle and law are to be understood in terms of God's loving heart that always seeks to bless rather than punish.

"Keep the sabbath by ceasing all manual labor"—unless doing so lets unnecessary harm come to man or beast you could have rescued; the exception you make on a given sabbath to "work your head off" to save that soul from harm is not a sinful abandonment of the sabbath law. You were dealing with an extraordinary set of circumstances. You will return to your customary practice when those circumstances pass.

"Stay married to your non-philandering mate until death separates you"—unless your spouse is making it impossible for you to live your Christian faith with godly dignity and lead your children to know Christ. If you and your children are at risk because of his drug use or abusive behaviors, divorce may be necessary in order to protect yourselves from the immediate or long-term harm he is inflicting on you. You are not being unfaithful to your vows or abandoning your husband; you are trying to live with a modicum of God's peace in your life under extraordinary conditions you did not create. Get out of there before you get killed, have to see your children get caught up in his addictive behaviors, or become party to denying them the gospel.

CHAPTER SEVEN

PAUL ON DIVORCE AND REMARRIAGE / PART 2

The importance of 1 Corinthians 7 to the pastoral application of Scripture to troubled marriages was explained in the previous chapter. Marriage is honorable, and celibacy is not somehow more spiritual. To those who were married at Corinth, Paul quoted the words of Jesus about fidelity within this covenant commitment. He also acknowledged the difficulty of making marriage work under extreme stress and faced the likelihood that some non-Christian mates would not be willing to continue living with a believer who was living his or her allegiance to Christ with commitment. Thus he opposed divorce but granted that it sometimes happened. With apostolic authority and pastoral love, he counseled against hasty remarriage—even encouraged some to consider remaining unmarried for the sake of kingdom service. For those who did not have this gift and calling, he recognized the importance of remarriage to avoid succumbing to sexual temptation.

Application of the Peace Principle (1 Cor 7:25-28)

At this point, Paul introduces still another group in addition to the four already named—"virgins" (Gk, *parthenos*). Technically, as with the widows (v.8) as well, they could have been addressed under the broader term "unmarried" that he has used already at vs. 8 and 11. But he reserves this group for last in view of the importance some at Corinth had attached to celibacy as the spiritually superior lifestyle for Christians living in a decadent environment. Of all persons, those who have never been married are the ones to be encouraged to embrace perpetual celibacy—if, indeed, it pleases God more than the married state. Is asceticism the Christian answer to sexual immorality?

Paul's response to such a possibility was neither to endorse nor to condemn. In a word, he answered, "It depends. There is no 'rule' to answer your question. There is no 'law' to enjoin a course of conduct. You live in the grace-environment made possible by Christ and must choose the life situation most appropriate to honoring him under your present circumstances. For some of you, celibacy would be the preferred option; for others, marriage is the better choice. Choose wisely—in light of the principle I have just articulated."

Given an uncertain situation before the Christians at Corinth, it was important for everyone to live in God's peace. Or, to say it in a variety of ways: Be wary of taking on new responsibilities. Don't bite off more than you can chew. Avoid entangling alliances. Stay out of uncharted waters. Or, to summarize what can now be discerned as a theme through this chapter, *remain as you are* (vs.8,11,17-24).

I do not know what the "impending crisis" of v.26a was. Some scholars understand it to refer to Paul's mistaken view that the coming of Christ was just around the corner. Others argue for an impending persecution about which we know nothing else. And still others see it as a way of speaking about the particularly distressing and hostile moral environment of Corinth. For our purposes, it is not necessary to form an opinion about what was in view. It is enough simply to know that special circumstances call for careful deliberation, urgent prayer, and great humility. All other factors being equal, wisdom says, "Do nothing until the smoke clears." Or, in Paul's thematic language, "Remain as you are until the crisis before you resolves."

David had done well in his medical practice, and Sue had done a good job with their two children. The success of his practice had allowed her to be a full-time mom. She had enjoyed being the primary nurturer in the lives of their two sons. With the younger one in school now, she finally had time to pursue a few of the things she had postponed for the sake of the children.

She had played on her high school tennis team, and the first thing she wanted to do was to take up the game again. She had no trouble convincing David it would be a good idea. He sometimes played tennis with the preacher from their church and liked the idea of playing mixed doubles with his wife.

David noticed changes in Sue's behavior over the next year. She was withdrawn, and he thought it might have something to do with both of their children being in school. Was she missing her nurturing role with them? He soon decided that was not the issue, for she seemed to be less and less involved with them in the evenings. She had to be asked to help with homework. Something was wrong, but David couldn't figure it out.

He was caught completely off-guard when Sue told him she was in love with the tennis pro at the club who had given her lessons. They had been having an affair from within a few weeks of staring her tennis lessons with him, and she was leaving David for him. She refused David's plea for them to get help and counseling. Sue said she was in love and would never look back.

Quiet introvert that he was, David had his lawyer work things out with Sue's attorney. Their friends at church were shocked when word of their split became known. David and Sue went their separate ways, and Sue moved about 25 miles away. She and her lover got married a few months after the divorce. Although she and David had joint custody of the two children, she gladly agreed for their primary residence to be with their father.

Seven years later, David had met someone and was dating quite seriously. He asked the preacher with whom he once had played tennis about performing a quiet wedding ceremony for them. He said he would have to know more about David's divorce and the circumstances leading up to it. He specifically asked David to provide him proof that Sue had broken up their marriage with an affair.

David was horrified by the demand. He told the preacher that he would not indulge his curiosity or scruples by lowering himself to slander his former wife. "She is still the mother of my children," he said, "and I am not going to open that *can of worms at this point in their young lives. I have no need to embarrass my former wife, and I will not further confuse and hurt my children."*

David and his fiancée were soon married by a local judge. Although his wife would like to attend church, David tells her repeatedly that he has no desire to do so any longer.

With no direct word from Jesus to quote—since this was, in fact, a situation unique to the Corinthians and in which some were being pressured to embrace asceticism—Paul spoke with apostolic authority to apply the principle he had just outlined to the issues at hand (v.25; cf. v.12). His "opinion" (NRSV) or "judgment" (NIV) was that the live-in-God's-peace principle translated as follows for never-married persons: "It is well for you to remain as you are" (v.26).

However, it should be emphasized, this is what the apostle has counseled along the way for *everyone* at Corinth, regardless of his or her status as a divorced (v.8a), widowed (v.8b), or married (v.10) person. Specifically, any man "bound to a wife" (i.e., married) should "not seek to be free" (i.e., divorce her); any man "free from a wife" (i.e., divorced) ought "not seek a wife" (i.e., get married). Thus v. 27 has counseled a general course of wait-and-see patience. But would everyone have the self-control necessary for an open-ended time of restraint? Earlier, you may recall, Paul had acknowledged that divorced and widowed persons "aflame with passion" might not be able to delay marriage indefinitely; under that circumstance of compromised self-control, "they should marry" (v.8). If those were persons whose divorce or bereavement perhaps preceded their conversion to Christ, what about baptized persons who had divorced since their conversion? Paul had earlier given them the advice not to get divorced or, if they went ahead with a marital separation, to remain unmarried or be reconciled (vs. 10-11). But was that instruction with only two options (i.e., reconcile or remain single) Paul's "pastoral counsel" or an "apostolic edict"? We might debate that question but for his explicit statement: "Are you bound to a wife? Do not seek to be free. Are you free from a wife? Do not seek a wife. *But if you marry, you do* not *sin, and if a virgin marries, she does* not *sin.*"

Language could hardly be clearer. Neither the person who has never been married (i.e., *parthenos*) nor the person who has been married but subsequently divorced (i.e., *agamos*[29]) would sin by getting married. Both might be using poor judgment under the "impending crisis" at Corinth. Both might live to regret the decision. Both might later say they made a mistake in doing so. But the apostle declared that it would *not* be a sin. We should be content to let the Bible speak on this and must avoid stigmatizing those who have exercised a right to remarry that a Spirit-guided apostle affirmed.

Peter and LaShandra met through an Internet chat room. She was outgoing, bright, and personable; he was shy, bright, and highly introverted. But they somehow "clicked" with each other and continued to chat several times every day.

They set up their first face-to-face meeting in St. Louis. LaShandra made a work trip there for a week of training, and Peter joined her on Friday for the weekend. He spent lavishly. He showered her with gifts. Their time together was supercharged with sex, and they parted with a commitment to stay in touch.

The Internet was their lifeline. There were not only text messages but photos. Peter was particularly eager to have nude photos of LaShandra, and she eventually began supplying explicit and graphic shots to satisfy him.

On their third personal encounter, Peter met her in Knoxville, took her directly from the airport to the County Clerk's Office, and began filling out an application for a marriage license. LaShandra filled out her part of the application as well. Within three hours of landing at the airport, the two were husband and wife.

She had the better job, so Peter moved to her city after giving two-week notice. He found work quickly. And they enjoyed the shocked looks on people's faces as they told family, work associates, and LaShandra's friends of their marriage. The first few months were a virtual whirlwind of activity. The sex was exciting.

By the six-month mark, things were terrible. They had nothing in common. She worked in retail furniture sales for a high-end company; he worked wherever he could and changed jobs fairly frequently. His personality alienated them from her friends; he had no friends in a city he had never visited before moving there. Lacking the need to chat via the Internet, the husband-wife duo hardly talked at all. Twenty-seven months after their impromptu wedding, they filed for divorce. "We don't have anything in common," she told the attorney. An uncontested divorce was granted.

Is LaShandra a candidate for hearing the gospel from your church? Is Peter? How would either of them be received? Would learning his story a few months after he started attending your church change the nature of the reception he got?

The way Paul handles the issue of remarriage seems to me to offer an insight we sometimes miss in all the biblical texts about divorce and remarriage. The Bible nowhere presumes that remarriage is sinful. To the contrary, it everywhere assumes that anyone who is not married is both likely to marry and permitted to do so. The moral failure surrounding the person in question is not that he or she would want to marry, be part of a family, and share intimate companionship with another. The moral failure is when one does not invest in a marriage, nurture her mate, or show grace to his partner in forgiving and healing wounds. Contrary to the idea of some that divorce might be unfortunate but remarriage is positively sinful, the gist of the biblical information points to an opposite view. When one seeks and obtains a divorce for some trivial reason, he sins against God and his mate and adulterates his marriage covenant; when and if he chooses to marry again, he must regard the new marriage as a holy commitment and take care not to repeat an earlier breach of marital faithfulness.

Time Is Growing Short (1 Cor 7:29-35)

The problem in identifying the "impending crisis" (v.26) at Corinth has already been acknowledged. It is the language of this section to the effect that "the appointed time has grown short" (v.29a) and "the present form (*schema*) of this world is passing away" (v.31b) that leads some to conclude Paul expected Jesus to return at any moment. I leave it to the textual scholars to debate what Paul had in mind. For my purpose as a theologian trying to understand the apostle's attitude toward divorce and remarriage, it is sufficient to say that he knew that the lives of his spiritual charges at Corinth were always in danger of embracing the immediate without due consideration of the long-term. That is true of Christians in every generation and culture, is it not?

The thrust of his plea is that Christians must always be "anxious about the affairs of the Lord, how to please the Lord" above all else. In the words of Jesus, a disciple's responsibility is to "strive first for the kingdom of God and his righteousness" in the assurance that the things necessary to human life and wellbeing "will be given to you as well" (Matt 6:33).

The reason why "remain as you are" seemed to be the right pastoral counsel for Paul to give the Corinthians was his concern to keep them from getting their lives enmeshed with worldly things to the neglect of spiritual concerns. While all of us "use the world" in the sense of living in it, we must avoid the temptation of thinking the world and its passing concerns are ultimate. Marriage (v.29), mourning (v.30a), celebrating (v.30b), buying (v.30c), owning (v.30c)—all these things are appropriate in life's various seasons, but they must not be allowed to get us off course with life's essential goal. In Paul's opinion, that was not the time to expand one's responsibilities by initiating new ventures—but, to the contrary, to pull in and to focus on duties already at hand. The implications of this for marriage should be apparent.

If one were to choose to begin a family at that point, an unmarried man would be inviting a host of "anxieties." And those anxieties would be less about kingdom mission than about "how to please his wife" (vs.32-33). Perhaps it is too much, however, to say that they would be "less" about the kingdom. We should be content with Paul simply to say that the man's interests would be "divided" (v.34a). It would be the same with a woman trying to learn how "to please her husband" (v.34c)—whether she was a woman who had never been married before (*parthenos*), a widow (*chera*), or a divorcee (*agamos*). Even so, Paul said all this as counsel rather than command: "I say this for your own benefit, not to put any restraint upon you, but to promote good order and unhindered devotion to the Lord" (v.35).

Paul's Final Thoughts (1 Cor 7:36-39)

The way this chapter has run may have been very unsatisfying for many of its original recipients at Corinth. Remember, some had apparently embraced asceticism and celibacy as the only proper response to Corinthian depravity. Their maxim was this: "It is well for a man not to touch a woman." By contrast, the Pauline rule of thumb was expressed this way: "In view of the impending crisis, it is well for you to remain as you are." Celibacy is not spiritually superior to the married life. Marriage is not a form of moral compromise for the spiritually weak, and the satisfaction of sexual passion in marriage is holy in the eyes of God. The potentially "unsatisfying" nature of all this for some at Corinth would be that it had not steered the church in the direction of ascetic faith.

The way this chapter runs leaves many who have read it after the first century feeling unsatisfied as well. There have been ascetic Christians across the centuries who have not appreciated the Pauline "privileges" throughout the chapter. There have been legalistic interpreters whose desire to read every biblical imperative as an inflexible rule has left them bewildered. And, unfortunately, there have been countless wounded and angry Christians who have needed to see their former spouses "pay for what they did" to them who have been frustrated by Paul's concessions about remarriage and what that has allowed their despised ex-husband or former wife to do in getting on with life after a rancorous divorce.

The statement about being "holy in body and spirit" in the middle of v.34 may have set the stage for Paul's concluding lines. First, against the uncertainty someone might have—influenced, no doubt, by those who were stressing celibacy—about following through with a marriage plan, Paul goes at the matter from still another angle. Yes, "remain as you are" is good advice for the engaged persons at Corinth (v.37); under the circumstances, it would be the preferred course (v.38). Again, though, that is what Paul has told everyone at Corinth—whether single (and presumably not yet engaged), married to another Christian, married to a non-Christian, divorced, or widowed. So why should he be expected to say anything different to the engaged person? Indeed, he gave his explicit permission for such persons to proceed with their wedding plans. "If his passions are strong and so it has to be, let him marry as he wishes; it is no sin. Let them marry" (v.36). If the initial reassurance of this statement was for the man and his betrothed, the closing emphatic "let them marry" must have been for any who would try to make them feel spiritually inferior for acknowledging their passionate needs.

Finally, having already referred to widows as early as v.8, a final word reaffirms the right of someone whose mate has died to marry again (v.39a). Even so, the remain-as-you-are prompt is repeated yet again at v.40. The only new instruction added is at v.39b—where a widow is declared "free to marry anyone she wishes, only in the Lord." It would be difficult to understand this language as anything other than Paul's intimation that she would be better advised to marry someone from the Christian community at Corinth. Again, however, it would be violating both the structure and spirit of this chapter to make this into a law rather than pastoral counsel for people he loved deeply.

In offering a summary of Pauline teaching about divorce and remarriage[30], at least the following items should not be overlooked:

First, there is not a full-blown theology of marriage, family, human sexuality, and the like in Paul. Paul did not write as a would-be systematic theologian or family counselor. For example, he says precious little about child-rearing—except that church leaders should demonstrate their ability to nurture the church as God's spiritual family by showing themselves faithful in rearing their own biological offspring. He wrote occasional letters to answer questions and to address problems. Some of the problems he faced in his day dealt with divorce and remarriage; we should take cues from his method of dealing with them.

Second, marriage is not required of anyone, and the single life (i.e., choosing never to marry or deciding to remain single following a divorce or the death of a mate) should not be disparaged. Making unmarried persons the butt of jokes is not only unkind but may even pressure certain people toward ill-advised marriages. Churches should not only value and affirm single persons but be sure that Jew and Greek, slave and free, male and female, single and married, divorced and widowed are included in their life and ministry. This is considerably harder to do than most church leaders realize or admit.

Third, not only is the single life not to be disparaged, Paul taught that it has great practical value for certain things pertaining to the Kingdom of God. One thinks not only of the singular devotion to ministry by Jesus and Paul but also of John the Baptist, perhaps Lydia, or others who chose to forego marriage for the sake of undivided devotion to the Lord. Certain missionary postings or special ministries that would make nurturing time for a family difficult to come by would make sense of this choice.

Fourth, occasional Christian teachings or groups to the contrary notwithstanding, a celibate lifestyle is neither morally nor spiritually superior to marriage. Biblical texts such as 1 Timothy 4:3 inveigh against such ascetic doctrines and practices: "They forbid marriage and demand abstinence from foods, which God created to be received with thanksgiving by those who believe and know the truth."

Caroline and Harold had been married 43 years and nine days when he died of a massive stroke. Their two grown children came in from nearby cities where Sue was a pediatrician and Michelle was a patent attorney. With their own families in tow, both women tended to their mother, helped with arrangements for the funeral, and stayed for a few days beyond it. Their mother would be taken care of, for their father had retired a decade ago when he sold his company for several million dollars.

Both Sue and Michelle were pleased eight months later when their mother called and asked their "permission" to go to dinner with a nice man she had met. Alan had bought the house next door to where she and Harold had reared their daughters. He loved doing yard work and had helped Caroline prune a couple of dangerous limbs. A few days later, he had asked Caroline to dinner. Her daughters thought it was sweet that their mother had called to get their blessing for that first date. It was a good idea, they agreed, for they knew their mother to be an outgoing person who had handled her loneliness poorly.

One dinner became regular outings together. Alan made Caroline feel very special, and he was always a perfect gentleman. He had sold his half of a partnership in a C.P.A. firm, moved to the sunny South from Minnesota, and was enjoying his retirement. Caroline had been a very unexpected surprise. His life had been his work for over 20 years, for he and his wife had divorced after less than ten years of marriage.

Alan was a nominal Roman Catholic and seldom went to church. So he was more than willing to accept Caroline's invitation to attend Sunday worship with her. It was strange at first, but the people were friendly. Alan and Caroline were coming to have a lot in common.

Sue and Michelle could not be happier for their mother. On their occasional trips home, they got to know Alan and understood quickly why Caroline liked spending time with him. Almost one year to the day that they had met doing yard work, Alan proposed marriage. Caroline accepted—with one significant reservation.

Caroline had deep, deep roots in her church. Her faith was genuine, and it was central to her life. She and Alan talked about their different religious backgrounds, and they agreed to talk with Caroline's minister. Three Bible studies later, Alan told him he wanted to "join the church"—language the preacher explained was not really appropriate. "Jesus adds people to his church," the minister explained. Alan didn't quite follow the explanation, but he accepted it.

Alan understood that his infant baptism would not be accepted by Caroline's church, and he had no objection to getting immersed. Because Sue and Michelle wanted to be present, it was set for the next weekend. It was a joyous event as new friends and soon-to-be new family hugged Alan and congratulated him.

One of the elders of his new church said he needed to speak with him privately before he left the building. Thinking it was for a time of prayer together, he agreed and worked his way to the small conference room the elder had identified. The minister and two other elders were at the table when Alan and Caroline walked in and took seats across the table from them.

"Our minister has shared your history with us, Alan," began the elder who had asked for the meeting. "We are happy you have been attending this church, and we are delighted you have been baptized into Christ. Now, as elders of this church, we have to tell you that you and Sue can't go through with this marriage we've heard about. Her husband died, and she is free to remarry. But you are divorced without scriptural grounds and would be living in adultery if you were ever marry again. You and Sue can be members of this church, but we will be forced to withdraw the church's fellowship from the two of you if you get married."

Alan sat stunned and disbelieving, while Sue began to cry—and seethe. She got up, asked Alan to take her home, and whispered to him as they walked onto the parking lot, "I'll never set foot on this property again as long as I live."

Fifth, marriage is honorable and should be regarded as a holy relationship to be encouraged and nurtured by Christians. It is not a concession to human weakness but part of the original, Edenic plan for human happiness. The family unit not only prevents immorality and provides for procreation of the human race but provides life's most intimate human companionship between adults, life's safest nurturing atmosphere for children, and life's most secure laboratory for personal spiritual growth.

Sixth, divorce is not part of the divine ideal. To the contrary, divorce represents a departure from God's will and always attests to sin. Since the essence of marriage is covenanting between a man and a woman, the repudiation of one's marital vows either by sexual infidelity or refusal to live in constant concern for one's mate constitutes adultery (i.e., covenant-breaking). Therefore Paul quotes Jesus to the effect that neither a husband nor wife is ever to take the initiative to disrupt covenant love and faithfulness.

Seventh, though not ideal, divorce is sometimes appropriate for a Christian who is married to an unbeliever. While God would use the believer's presence in a family to bless that person's mate and any children born to them, that blessing must be received and cannot be forced. Indeed, God considers the unbelieving members of such families set apart for faith through the Christian's presence. In situations where there are extreme forms of opposition to the Christian in such a marriage, the unbelieving mate may choose to divorce him or her. In situations of abuse, alcoholism, or child endangerment, the moral equivalent of divorce (i.e., unfaithfulness to one's covenant responsibilities) occurs and may be recognized by the courts at the instigation of the believing spouse as an act of self-defense. Since marriage is a voluntary covenant, the believer—who is always called to God's peace in his or her life—is no longer bound by matrimonial commitments and is not guilty of covenant-breaking in the matter.

Eighth, although divorce is no part of God's ideal for human life, it is nevertheless a reality in human experience. Paul acknowledges that divorce happens without ever diminishing the seriousness of covenant-breaking. Sometimes, as just noted, unbelieving partners refuse to live with their Christian mates and cause their marriages to fail. In other instances, marriages fail for a variety of reasons that involve sin on the part of one or both adult partners to the relationship.

Ninth, whenever a Christian is involved in a divorce, it is typically wise for him or her to remain unmarried for a time in order to avoid the snare of an ill-formed relationship. Marriages formed "on the rebound" are particularly risky. There needs to be a time of healing and renewal. If reconciliation becomes a viable option during that season of renewal, it can be pursued.

Tenth, Paul accepts the fact that remarriage is likely to occur in the lives of most people who divorce. Aside from the caveat already specified about seeking reconciliation when possible, divorced persons who remarry do not sin by doing so and should not be excluded from the life of the church. Even in cases where special circumstances seem to make marriage inadvisable—whether one's first, second, or subsequent marriage—marriage is holy and not to be forbidden.

Eleventh, without regard to the circumstances of one's divorce, the right of remarriage is explicitly granted by the apostle (i.e., "If you marry, you do not sin," v.28) and may be essential to the completion of one's spiritual recovery from a failed marriage.

Twelfth, Paul does not envision an ecclesial court or its equivalent to investigate, judge, or otherwise pry into the pain of one's marital past. Church leaders in our own time should urge fidelity within marriage, offer resources to assist struggling relationships, and support post-divorce reconciliation when possible.

CHAPTER EIGHT

SOME QUESTIONS THAT ARISE

The exploration of a subject so complex and difficult as divorce and remarriage is sure to generate questions. From the oral delivery of different parts of this material, I have learned there are some questions that occur with great predictably. Wrestling with them is part of the theological process. How does the Word of God relate to a specific time and place that may be very different from those in which a given instruction was given? How do we balance holy standards and real life in a fallen world? How may church leaders demonstrate compassionate grace without compromising the truths God has revealed?

This chapter will state and reply to some of the most frequent issues that are raised when this topic is on the floor. As with every other part of this book, I will give the best response of which I am capable. Never once will I assume to have the final word on these issues. My hope is not that I could say everything that needs to be said in a definitive way but that I might contribute something to your own process of thinking through some aspect of the subject.

Question: "Permission to get divorced?"

Aren't you afraid that someone reading this book could interpret what you have said as their "permission" to leave a bad marriage that could yet be saved with prayer, effort, and help?

Yes. I seldom present any of this material without voicing this very fear. There are always people whose marriages are shaky and whose commitment to saving them is minimal. I would be foolish not to think that someone in that situation might not think the possibility of pardon and renewal for divorcees is just the loophole he or she has been searching to find.

Do we not face the same possibility with any number of human behaviors? Should we not teach that God forgives lying, lest someone hear that as her permission to tell lies? Should we not teach that the blood of Christ is powerful enough to cleanse a murderer's guilt for fear someone might hear that as his go-ahead to take someone's life? The list could go on indefinitely, but you surely see the point. It is not an acceptable strategy for discouraging sin to withhold the gospel's message of forgiveness—forgiveness that is full and absolute.

The teaching of the Roman Catholic Church that divorce is not allowed and that divorce and remarriage excludes one from Holy Communion seems not to have put a stop to marital failure among Catholics; it has simply generated what many regard as a dishonest form of gamesmanship about the "annulment" of long-duration marriages with several children. Neither has the teaching of many Churches of Christ that divorce may be a necessary evil under extreme circumstances but that remarriage is sinful and causes one to "live in adultery" put a stop to divorce in our congregations; it has produced the need on the part of some to slander a former mate or to lie about one's own sin that helped doom the marriage to failure.

In offering the gospel's message of genuine forgiveness to sinners—no matter the nature of the sin—we certainly do not invite people to sin. We simply offer the message of hope that is God's "good news" to everyone. If someone's heart is so corrupt and hardened as to hear the gospel as license to sin, it is not the message that is at fault.

Question: "Are you divorced?"

In my experience, people who are soft on divorce and remarriage are trying to justify themselves. Are you divorced? If so, what caused your divorce?

Welcome to the world of new experiences! No, I am not divorced. My parents were married for more than 50 years before my father's death. My wife and I have three grown and married children—none of whom is divorced.

Perhaps a deeper-level response to this question, however, is to plead for more civility and respect among people who disagree with each other. The assumption that one who takes a contrary view "has an agenda," is hiding something, or trying to justify his or her personal sin is both unfair and unkind. It is altogether possible that one can disagree with another person in good faith and as a result of serious study of the Scriptures. In my case, I was taught, accepted, and defended a very rigid view that allowed remarriage only to widowed persons and for those who were innocent parties in situations of divorce for sexual infidelity. While preaching a series of sermons on the Ten Commandments years ago, my study of the seventh commandment—especially as that commandment relates both to the story of King David and to Jesus' comments on it in the Sermon on the Mount—put me in the awkward position of inconsistency with what I had always heard and believed about divorce. For three years after that point, I invested considerable time and energy into restudying the biblical text. I decided I had been mistaken. Changing my mind on the subject had nothing to do with a change of marital status; it had everything to do with trying to be fair with the biblical materials.

Finally on this point, the way this question ends (i.e., "If so, what caused your divorce?") reflects—though unintentionally I am sure—something of a mean spirit toward divorced persons. Do we really have the right to interrogate divorced people? Is it godly to pry into one's past? Applying for employment with a government agency that is privy to national security secrets is one thing; the applicant knows his or her background will be scrutinized. Presenting oneself for baptism or for membership with a local church is quite different; a community of the forgiven is about love, accountability, and nurture of one's new life in Christ.

Question: "What does repentance require?"

If somebody has divorced for a trivial cause and then married again, your book says they are in an adulterous relationship. How can two people repent of being in an adulterous relationship and stay in it? Don't they have to end their relationship? I know that anybody who stole a car would have to give it back in order to show the "fruits of repentance"—and I don't think marriage is any different.

With all due respect, this question is so poorly framed that it is all the more difficult to answer.

First, this book does *not* speak of divorced and remarried persons as being in "an adulterous relationship." I do not know what to make of the term. It isn't a biblical term or concept. This book speaks of adultery—breaking faith in one's marital covenant, usually by means of sexual infidelity.

This book has quoted both Jesus and Paul to the effect that anyone who divorces and remarries for some trivial justification is guilty of adultery in doing so. As was pointed out in the comments on Mark 10 in Chapter Five of this book, Jesus said that adultery is "against" the companion put away and not "with" the new mate. Thus the warranted conclusion seems to be that adultery relates to the actions that go into ending a marriage, not the ones that issue from a remarriage.

Second, repentance does not demand what is impossible. No more than murderers can repent of their actions by bring the dead person back to life can someone who has been guilty of adultery against someone unscramble the eggs of a broken relationship. It certainly is not right or reasonable to suggest that the "solution" is a second divorce. That would be the classic illustration of how two wrongs do not make a right. Repenting of adultery means feeling genuine remorse for anything one may have contributed to the failure of a past marriage and determining not to repeat those mistakes in the new one. The fruits of repentance in the new relationship would be love, patience, and commitment by the renewing power of the Holy Spirit.

Third, although I have heard the analogy used repeatedly, it is a mistaken analogy when someone compares property crimes to relationship failures. Repentance involving money or property certainly entails a duty of restitution. To repent of one's failure in a marriage does not allow "returning" or "reclaiming" a person, as if people were property to be exchanged. It might be helpful to re-read the material in Chapters II and III about the reason behind the Deuteronomy 24 duty to give the divorced woman a "certificate of divorce." It was designed to prevent men from treating women as property. Without realizing it, people who suggest "taking back" or "giving back" a person are demeaning the significance of what it means to be a human being in the image of God.

Question: "What about Romans 7:2-3 on this topic?"

A dear friend whom I respect highly is a member of a church that refuses remarriage to all divorced persons—even the innocent party in a divorce due to sexual infidelity—on the basis of Paul's statement about adultery in Romans 7:2-3. How do you interpret this text? Why didn't you include it in your survey of Paul's teaching on divorce and remarriage?

It is correct that some Christians base their view that opposes all remarriages except for widows/widowers on the basis of this text: "Thus a married woman is bound by the law to her husband as long as he lives; but if her husband dies, she is discharged from the law concerning the husband. Accordingly, she will be called an adulteress if she lives with another man while her husband is alive. But if her husband dies, she is free from that law, and if she marries another man, she is not an adulteress." From this statement, it is concluded that "anybody with a living former husband or wife" would be committing adultery to marry following a divorce.

I disagree with this interpretation for several reasons. First, it clearly contradicts what both Jesus and Paul taught in the passages studied earlier. Paul was not a careless thinker or writer and would not be guilty of such flagrant self-contradiction. Second, it is not correct that "a married woman is bound by the law to her husband as long as he lives"—regardless of any special circumstances that might arise. The Law of Moses explicitly identifies a number of situations under which divorce might and—even in a few cases we examined—should occur. Paul knew the Torah and the Prophets and was aware of these.

In Romans 7, Paul is not addressing issues of divorce and remarriage for his readers. He is making an argument about the relationship of his fellow-Jews to the Law of Moses and Christ. "Do you not know, brothers and sisters—for I am speaking to those who know the law—that the law is binding on a person only during that person's lifetime?" (v.1) He illustrates his point by saying the covenant of marriage works the same way; that is, death breaks the marital bond. He concludes: "In the same way, my friends, you have died to the law through the body of Christ, so that you may belong to another, to him who has been raised from the dead in order that we may bear fruit for God" (v.4).

Just as the marital covenant binds two people to each other, so did Yahweh's covenant with the Jews bind them together—as bridegroom to bride, a metaphor used in the Old Testament. Yet Paul has argued already in Romans 6 that all who have turned to Christ "were baptized into Christ's death" (v.4) and are to "reckon yourselves dead to sin" (v.11). Union with Christ's death in baptism not only implied a death to sin but to right-standing with God through the Law of Moses as well. It is the resurrected Christ who gives life to those who have died to sin; it is the living Christ who gives right-standing to Jews and Gentiles alike in one body. As he writes elsewhere: "For through the law I died to the law, so that I might live to God. I have been crucified with Christ" (Gal 2:19). Therefore, Paul's argument runs, neither he nor his Jewish readers at Rome should consider themselves adulterous (i.e., covenant-breakers, unfaithful persons) by virtue of their present status as Christ-followers.

The apostle's use of the general principle that marriage for life is terminated by one partner's death and confers the right to marry another is therefore an illustration of how Jews could become Christians without betraying Moses or committing a form of spiritual adultery. I did not include this text in the chapters on Paul's teaching about divorce and remarriage for the simple reason that it is not relevant. It doesn't bring up the subject of divorce. In those texts that do surface the issue of divorce, the Bible makes it clear that a legal dissolution of marriage has the same effect that death has to end the relationship between the persons involved.

Question: "What is 'divorce' anyway?"

What does God recognize as divorce? Are people who have gone through the court process of divorce somehow "still married in the eyes of God"? Do they remain married to each other until one of them becomes another person's sexual partner in a new marriage?

Two people are married when the civil law to which they are accountable says they are married.

From culture to culture, even from state to state within the United States, the statutes vary. In general, we may say that when an unmarried man and an unmarried woman freely choose to marry, comply with the appropriate statutes (e.g., secure a marriage license), and covenant before an appropriate authority (e.g., minister, justice of the peace), they are married. Within their legal union, they have certain rights and obligations. Similarly, two people are divorced when the civil law to which they are subject says they are divorced.

No more can people be "married in the eyes of God" without good-faith compliance with the relevant civil statutes can anyone think they are "married in the eyes of God" when the same civil authority has declared their marriage dissolved. Nobody who is divorced under the relevant laws of the time and place where he or she lives is somehow mystically linked in marriage to the former wife or husband.

Question: "Why isn't divorce sinful—only remarriage?"

What I have always been taught is that divorce may sometimes be a "necessary evil" but that a person's remarriage is "adultery" because that person is still married to the first companion in God's sight. Why is this so? Is it because of the sex involved in the second relationship?

In my opinion, this question is hopelessly garbled—for a variety of reasons. First, see the question immediately prior to this one about legal proceedings claiming to dissolve a marriage and two people somehow still being married in God's sight. People who get valid legal divorces are not married to anybody. They are unmarried, single, or divorced—not married in the eyes of humans or of God. The Gospel of John, for example, tells of an encounter between Jesus and a Samaritan woman. He suggested that she get her husband to join their conversation, and she said she had none. This was Jesus' reply to her: "You are right in saying, 'I have no husband'; for you have had five husbands, and the one you have now is not your husband" (John 4:16-18). She was not somehow still married either to the first or fifth of her previous husbands. And the fact that she was living with a sixth man didn't make him her husband, for there had been no legally recognized covenant formed between them. Second, it stands both the biblical materials and common sense on their heads to reason that divorce is somehow reluctantly tolerable but remarriage is sinful.

In Scripture, "adultery" is a sin directly tied to the breakup of a previous marriage and only indirectly associated with the formation of a subsequent marital union. As evidence for this view, notice that Mark 10:11 says "Whoever divorces his wife and marries another commits adultery *against* her [i.e., the first wife]" by breaking his promise to remain with her until death rather than "commits adultery *with* her [i.e., the second wife]." In view of the biblical data, then, one is an adulterer (i.e., covenant-breaker) who dissolves a marriage—whether or not a remarriage ever occurs. The Bible typically uses "divorce" and "divorce and remarriage" as equivalent terms because the presumption is that remarriage will follow a divorce. Our own reasoning tells us the same thing. A couple whose divorce decree bears today's date has not sinned by filing papers, going before a judge, and receiving a formal decree. Whatever objective guilt they bear relates directly to things each partner may have done to undermine and destroy their relationship.

In summary, the so-called "Matthean exception" says that someone divorcing a mate who has been guilty of sexual infidelity incurs no guilt for that action (Matt 19:9). There is also a "Pauline exception" for a Christian who divorces his or her non-Christian mate who is unwilling to live with someone who is putting the Kingdom of God first in his or her life (1 Cor 7:15). To divorce under any other circumstance—whether for what I would call trivial causes (i.e., "We just didn't get along" or "We're not compatible"), for serious-but-not-infidelity reasons (i.e., alcoholism, abuse, etc.), or for sexual infidelity (i.e., as the "guilty party" who was unfaithful to his or her vows)—is to sin. The specific name of the sin committed in such cases is *adultery* (i.e., covenant-breaking). Even so, adultery is not an unpardonable sin. [Note: See the next question.]

Question: "Is divorce unpardonable?"

Is divorce somehow different than other sins? Is the adultery or covenant-breaking element somehow unpardonable?

No sin is beyond the reach of God's grace! Any sin repented of and offered to God for pardon will be forgiven by the limitless efficacy of Christ's blood. Fornication, child molestation, rape, sodomy, bestiality, polygamy—all may be forgiven. And adultery is neither a greater sin than these nor is it beyond the power of God to forgive. "Fornicators, idolaters, *adulterers*, male prostitutes, sodomites, thieves, the greedy, drunkards, revilers, robbers—none of these will inherit the kingdom of God. *And that is what some of you used to be*. But you were washed, you were sanctified, you were justified in the name of the Lord Jesus Christ and in the Spirit of our God" (1 Cor 6:9c-11). The italicized words in the text just quoted prove that adultery is not unpardonable.

Question: "Should I divorce my new partner?"

I was unfaithful to my wife seven years ago. She divorced me, and I married the woman with whom I was having the affair four and one-half years ago. Although we get along well and have a son, I am overwhelmed now by a sense of guilt for what I did. My new wife and I agree that we were inexcusably wrong in our sin. The preacher we went to said we must get a divorce and that my only option for being married is for my first wife to take me back. But she got married last year. So what should we do?

Yes, you committed adultery against your wife and entered a second marriage you had no right to form. It is to your credit that you are neither justifying yourself nor blaming your first wife for what happened. But the counsel you have been given is horribly mistaken, and I hope you will reject it for a more biblical course.

Whatever moral and spiritual offenses you and your present wife were guilty of will be (or have been) forgiven when repented of and washed clean by the blood of Jesus Christ. As in so many cases of repentance following divorce, your remorse over the past does not undo or fix the harm already done. [Note: If your remorse had come after your divorce and prior to your remarriage, I would give different advice here. I would plead for you and your ex-wife to seek counsel that might help you reconcile your differences and remarry. That advice is now moot—although the preacher you saw may think he is giving you some form of that Pauline counsel.]

Your repentance now means that you are forgiven. And the responsibility of a penitent person is never to repeat the sin for which you have been pardoned. But that is exactly what you would be doing, if you listen to the advice you have been given. If you divorce your present wife and/or encourage your former wife to leave her husband to remarry you, you will have tried to correct one unauthorized divorce with two more! The old adage that two wrongs—or, by my count, *three* in this scenario—don't make a right should be kept in mind here.

Repentance does not enable someone to "unscramble eggs" (i.e., undo harm already done, put back together a shattered relationship) but accepts responsibility, confesses sin, accepts forgiveness, and pledges to seek God's help never to commit the same transgression in the future. In the case of someone who remarries following a divorce, the duty of repentance from adultery (i.e., covenant-breaking) is to try to understand what one's behavior did to break up the previous marriage (e.g., bad temper, adultery, financial irresponsibility), seek help to correct those out-of-control areas of one's heart and life (e.g., spiritual disciplines, counseling, support groups), devote one's new life and new relationship to God, and live the new marital relationship with greater maturity than the first. We must not require of people what Scripture does not. We must not make the lives of penitent people still more difficult.

Even in the *hyperbole* of the Sermon on the Mount, Jesus—who told lustful people to pluck out their eyes and greedy people to cut off their hands—did not tell the divorced-and-remarried adulterer to put away his new wife. Neither may we.

Question: "Take him back?"

My husband and I divorced seven months ago, after eight years of marriage and two children. He is alcoholic, abusive, and admits to multiple affairs. Last week he told me he has begun attending Alcoholics Anonymous, wants me to go to marriage counseling with him, and asked to move back home to work things out with me and the kids. I want to do the right thing as a Christian. And I want to help him get well. Should I take him back?

Not now! By no means should you allow him to "move back home" in the near future. For one thing, the two of you aren't married. For another, he has started on a recovery path that has a long, long way to go before you should consider trying to reconcile with him. And you should not expose yourself and your children to further heartache at his hands.

People can recover from alcoholism, abusive bad tempers, and sexual addiction—by God's empowering grace at work through the Holy Spirit who indwells his people. But recovery is seldom (if ever!) instantaneous. It is a long and challenging process of gradual transformation—usually with setbacks. If you can find it in your heart to do so, encourage your former husband to follow through with his commitments. If you are willing to consider reconciliation options in the future, let that be part of his motivation for getting well.

Probably the worst thing you could do for him is to forgive him in some naïve way, remarry him, and let him come home. He will be far more likely to revert to his old patterns of behavior. If the next several months go well, you can begin talking. If the next year or two go well, you might want to consider having a counselor help both of you size up your options. But your Christian duty to be forgiving does not obligate you to take him back. That is a decision to be made much later, depending on what you see among his fruits of repentance.

The Bible does not require a Christian to divorce an unfaithful spouse; forgiveness on the basis of love is always an option. Neither does the Bible require a Christian to take back a now-penitent spouse; possibilities for reconciliation are often quite complex and must be weighed very carefully over time.

Question: "Not 'worry so much' about getting divorced?"

I have dear friends whose marriage is in desperate trouble. I have never heard of anything quite so complex as the mess they have confided to me. Right now the only thing holding them together is their fear of what divorce might do to their two kids—and, to some degree, their fear of what would happen to them in our church. Who would have to leave? Who would get the church's support? Maybe I should just tell them not to worry so much about getting divorced, since they can both remarry later and perhaps be happy then.

Wow. That would be a terrible way to interpret the thesis of this book. Divorce *is* a terrible thing. Just ask anybody who has ever gone through one. And I for one am not beneath asking people to try to hold their marriages together "for the sake of the kids" because of the harm done to young lives when their mom and dad go separate ways. I'd suggest a very different strategy from telling them happiness is somewhere down the road after divorce. In fact, that is probably very poor advice to give most people whose marriages are in trouble. It is typically wiser to face and deal with relationship problems right now than to postpone them to the second or third marriage. Let me explain what I mean.

First, what I would urge you to do is to help the couple find resources they may not have tried yet to get help for their marriage. It is usually a good thing when a couple finally trusts someone enough to say, "Help! We're in real trouble!" The problem is that the friend, preacher, or church leader they trust is probably not a marriage therapist. That the problems look "hopeless" to you or me means very little about what God can do for humble, willing hearts who are now open to receiving his help. Christian counselors, marriage therapists, psychiatrists—there are people with specialized training who know how to help couples identify and address problems. God can use them as his ministers of healing.

Don't feel that you are abandoning them to ask them to go to a professional source for help. For example, I am a preacher and not a marriage therapist. This book is a theological study and not a means to resolving marital conflicts. When individuals or couples trust me enough to confide their problems, I pledge two things: (a) I will help you find competent help to deal with financial problems, sexual issues, or whatever the presenting problem seems to be, and (b) I will be your friend and cheerleader as you follow through with the process of working through those problems.

Second, divorce seldom solves problems. And I have known of several situations where it wasn't until the second or third marriage that a person discovered that. For example, a woman was contemplating her third divorce. This marriage had become as bad as the first two. And she thought this man was really different. (Neither of her previous marriages had ended by either partner's infidelity, and there was no accusation of infidelity in this case either.) Her lawyer asked her to talk with a minister she trusted before making her decision to file. When she said she didn't really know the minister at her own church, he suggested she talk with me. A few questions into the conversation made me think the problem was not with "the marriage" but with something going on deep inside her. She couldn't name anything terribly specific about either her husband or their relationship that seemed to say they couldn't make a go of things. When she agreed to let me ask a few questions about her early life experiences and what had shaped her view of life, she revealed the deep secret she had never shared with a living soul. She had been molested repeatedly over a period of several years by a family member when she was in her pre-teen years.

I immediately asked the sobbing woman to trust me to refer her to a female counselor I knew who had experience with helping women who have suffered sexual abuse as children. She entered a period of therapy, brought her husband into the process, and found the healing she had needed for years. If her attorney had simply filed the papers for her third divorce, that woman would probably be ready for her fourth by now. Her previous divorces were surely rooted in unresolved trauma from her childhood, but she had no idea what to do with her terrible secret that was destroying her. Each of the earlier divorces was a mere postponement of facing her real issue. Each had been a type of denial as to what was really going on with her. Each had been her way of running—when she didn't know what else to do.

Don't tell people not to worry about divorce. *Do* encourage them not to get divorced without trying everything possible to find a way to honor the commitments they have made.

Question: "Choosing Sides?"

The previous question mentioned the couple's fear of how their church would react to a divorce and whose side it would take. How does a church make the decision about which side to take when a divorce does occur?

I hate the idea of "taking sides" in a divorce. Does that sound like God? Does it sound like a godly thing for us to do? Why couldn't a church's leaders promise a couple not to choose sides—to love Bob and Mary, to help both of them get the assistance needed, and to remain spiritual family to them regardless of the outcome?

The idea that a church must side with one of the persons against the other brings the world's methods into the church. Paul said the people of God should work toward peace in marriage relationships (1 Cor 7:15b), yet churches sometimes—without meaning to do so, I hasten to add—introduce another layer of tension and strife by tempting the man and woman to seek sympathy and support from their church friends by denigrating the other. It would seem far better for a church to plead for reconciliation, do all within its power to support both husband and wife, and affirm the love of God for her or him as a person in God's own image—even if the marriage does not survive.

The next question is likely this: But how practical is that? Can a church continue to have fellowship with both people following a divorce?

If one (or both!) of the parties to a marriage is obviously responsible for harm to their relationship because of alcoholism, adultery, or neglect, a church should make its decisions about rebuke and future fellowship the same way it would in any situation. If the person repents, affirm God's pardon and encourage recovery. If he or she remains obstinate and impenitent, the issue at stake is not divorce so much as addiction, infidelity, or abandonment—now compounded by a divorce action. The New Testament makes it clear that the church is supposed to reflect God's holiness to the world. Anyone who is deliberate and headstrong about doing evil becomes subject to church discipline—ranging from prayer to rebuke to censure to excommunication from the body. In such an extreme case, the church has chosen the path of appropriate intervention over silence in the face of intentional sin.

But what about a less-extreme situation of good people who have made a good-faith attempt with prayer, counseling, and help from various resources—only to realize their marriage cannot survive? (Against the view that such a situation could never occur if the people really tried to save their relationship, I respectfully disagree. Reason, experience, and research in the discipline combine to say that some marriages fail simply because some people have been so emotionally impaired as to be incapable of healthy relationships. Practically all of us have known people who married because of a pregnancy, and many of these marriages will not survive because they were entered for inadequate reasons. Add to these the unions formed by persons too immature and too inexperienced with life to be able to choose a mate, and the number of otherwise good and decent people who nevertheless cannot keep a poor marriage together is frighteningly large.) It is possible for a church to love, receive, and nurture both parties after divorce occurs. I served a church for 27 years where this very thing happened without either person being rejected, abused, or otherwise made unwelcome in its congregational life. Godly elders with the heart of Christ must model this behavior toward fallible people in order for the larger church body to grasp the reality of redemptive love.

In such an atmosphere, growth on the part of both parties can take place. Insight, repentance, and spiritual clarity will emerge for them as believers. Following the principles outlined by Paul in 1 Corinthians 7, such persons are always to be encouraged not to rush into another relationship and certainly not to remarry quickly (v.11). Reconciliation may yet occur. Personal growth sometimes allows them to get back together, and I have presided at weddings of people over whose divorce I wept years before. On the other hand, personal growth may only serve to make it clear that their marriage was ill-advised from the start and that they could never reasonably choose each other as life partners. In such cases, these divorced persons may choose to marry again—but not remarry each other. Paul's words are appropriate to them that their choice to marry is not a sin (v.28).

Question: "Why a different standard for elders?"

Why did Paul specifically forbid someone who has been divorced to be an elder in the church? Is 1 Timothy 3:2 not clear that a church leader must be "married only once"? Doesn't that imply something for the church's general membership?

The NRSV reading "married only once" is more literally, as in the footnote, "the husband of one wife" or "the man of one wife." In other words, it doesn't quite mean "someone who has never been divorced" or "married only once."

Most scholars understand the Greek expression to mean that an elder is to model fidelity to his wife. That is, he is not to be a man of loose or questionable morals. He is not to be a flirt or tease. A married man should love his wife so obviously that no one who sees him around her would ever question his devotion to her. If this is not the correct meaning of the term, then not only persons who have been divorced but widowers who have remarried also are barred from serving the church as elder-shepherds.

Either a divorced-and-remarried man or a widowed-and-remarried man must, of course, prove his ability to lead in spiritual matters by establishing a solid Christian reputation over time.

Question: "How dare you!"

How dare you take the Bible and try to make it say that my husband has a right to get married and go on with his life after what he did to me and our children! We suffered. Why shouldn't he?

I think this isn't really a question at all. It seems more likely to be the angry—even vindictive—response of someone who has been wounded deeply by someone's sin.

I understand getting angry. I understand the natural human sentiment that "he should have to pay for what he did." And I believe there *are* consequences that will spill over into someone's life from the mistreatment and betrayal of others. In the universe of human experience, it is true that "what goes around comes around." But these are human sentiments and sayings—not explorations of the Word of God and expressions of the heart of Christ.

The point of this book is not to get people off the hook for their sin. It is to try to understand how Scripture views and wants us to deal with persons who are implicated by one particular sin.

Adultery, abuse, alcoholism, absenteeism, atheism, aggression—the gospel says they may all be forgiven. (Notice, please, that we are still only in first letter of the alphabet and the list is horribly incomplete even for that one letter!) While each of these offenses against God brings its own consequences, none of them requires a special penance or ongoing state of self-denial in order to be forgiven. Or is divorce the exception? Is celibacy a special penance for people who failed at marriage? Is singleness until death the ongoing state which, if violated, revokes God's pardon?

Perhaps in so intimate a human relationship as marriage above any other situation I can envision, we must be careful not to import anger, hatred, and the desire for retribution into our reading of Scripture.

Question: "If someone divorces, how long before remarriage?"

You have just cited Paul's counsel to divorced people. In Chapters VI and VII, you made a distinction between "pastoral counsel" and "absolute rule"—and that is helpful. But how long should someone wait after a divorce to consider remarriage? Should churches formulate policies about a minimum of two years, three years, etc.?"

Be careful! Questions of this sort reflect the fondness (perhaps I should say weakness) of religious people to want a set of rules that will cover everything. There is simply no way to set a policy for these situations. General guidelines have a way of becoming church policy and quickly morph into a rigid requirement.

In the study of 1 Corinthians 7 earlier, I made a case for Paul's common sense approach to divorce among believers in a fallen world: (a) Do everything reasonably possible to avoid divorce (vs.2,10,27a); (b) if you do choose to divorce your mate, stay single for a time in the hope of working out your problems and reconciling your relationship (vs.8,27b); (c) if you face the temptation of being "aflame with passion" as a divorcee, you should consider marriage (v.9); (d) if you should choose to marry again, you have not sinned by doing so (v.28a). How this process may unfold in particular life situations is not predictable, and it cannot be dictated by church policy. This is where church leaders should be sought for counsel, prayer, and practical guidance. It is also an instance where those leaders must proceed with caution. Giving what they consider to be mature counsel must not be confused with a divine command. Paul made it clear that one's choice to go against his judgment was not equivalent to violating God's will.

Question: "Should I officiate their wedding?"

I am a preacher, and a couple in their mid-30s has asked me to perform their marriage ceremony. They are both members of our church. So I agreed, blocked the date on my calendar, and asked them to enter a brief marriage-preparation course I share with all the couples whose weddings I officiate. In our second session, the woman referred to first marriage. I didn't know she had been divorced. Should I follow through with my commitment? How should I go about investigating the circumstances of her divorce in order to be sure she had a scriptural right to divorce her first mate?

I do not believe you have either the responsibility or the right to go on a "fishing expedition" in her life. If you were to do so, how would you know when you had all the facts? Would you still fear that she was putting herself in the best light or interpreting things with a selfish slant? Would you then try to interrogate her former husband in order to verify her version? Stop! Preaching the gospel and ministering Christ's love into human lives must not be confused with being a private investigator—or spiritual inquisitor.

I do, however, understand your dilemma. Your concern is to be faithful in your role as a minister. You don't want to ignore sin, if there is unrepented sin in her life that caused the previous marriage to fail. You don't want to appear to condone divorce or to take it lightly. You don't want the couple to enter this marriage without a clear determination to make it succeed. Again, I know of no policy or fixed rule for handling such situations. [Note: Please see the next question for follow-up on this.]

Question: "How do you personally handle these situations?"

From what you have just said, I presume you do not refuse to perform wedding ceremonies for people who have been married before. So how do you handle the subject, if it comes up?

Here is what I do when the issue of divorce surfaces—whether unexpectedly or because I know something of a person's previous life history.

"Sue, you mentioned your divorce. Without intending either to embarrass you or to cause pain, I would like to say something to that situation before we move on. Bob obviously knows about it, or you would not have brought it up in this setting. First, let me say the obvious. Divorce is painful and was never part of God's ideal for us. The Bible even says God 'hates divorce'—as practically everybody I know who has gone through a divorce does. Second, I have no intention of prying into your divorce or making a judgment about either it or you, Sue. I am a minister of the gospel of Christ, and my role is not that of a judge. Third, if there are issues still lingering from the heartache you went through in that divorce, Sue, I would like to help you lay them to rest for the sake of a future the two of you are hoping to share.

"Bob, if the two of you haven't talked through that event to your satisfaction, please do that at a private time between you. If you have had that conversation already and think I can help you with any of the things that surfaced, I will do my best to be helpful. [Here couples sometimes need to talk about shared custody of children, how the new person will participate in parenting duties, child support, school programs, etc.]

"Sue, if there are holdover issues from that marriage where you feel you were inadequate or failed, it is my place to affirm God's love and peace to you for anything and everything you have offered to him in repentance. Don't carry any unresolved guilt into this new marriage with Bob that might haunt you or become a problem in your relationship. If any of those issues still need 'repair' or 'healing,' there are good Christian counselors to help. If you were the victim of your former mate's unresolved issues or problem behaviors, you may need some help to put those behind you. You need to begin life with Bob without the fear that 'all men are alike.' It certainly won't be fair for him to have to earn a reluctant trust from you.

"I repeat: I am neither prying nor judging. I simply want both of you to feel comfortable about every aspect of who you are and who this person is you are about to marry. Old baggage from the past can become burdensome and harmful."

To the best of my knowledge, nobody has ever resented this rather typical statement I have made to scores of people in pre-marital settings. To say the least, none of the couples has ever walked out on me or said they didn't want me to be part of their wedding. Many of them have become close friends.

In response to this opening, some couples have simply looked at each other and nodded—signaling to me that they have done everything they feel is necessary with the subject. We move on. Others have said, "Thank you for pointing to the elephant in the room. Yes, we know there are [financial, emotional, child-rearing] issues we must face related to that divorce. And we wanted to ask your suggestion about how to deal with . . ." In a few instances, I have been able to help them directly; in many others, I have shared the names of two or three persons I trust who could advise them more appropriately.

There have also been situations where bringing up the subject of a past marital failure brought tears, confessions of confused feelings or anger over how churches treat divorced persons, and long teaching sessions. While never compromising the importance and sacredness of marriage, I have also taught about the heart of God the Loving Father. He wants the best for us and calls us to Plan A in our lives as his children. In the case of marriage, that means that he affirms its sacredness and warns us against breaking our marriage vows. When we fail in our marriage covenants, he calls us to repent and salvage the relationships whenever possible. When that cannot be done, he offers Plan B to his frail children. He redeems our lives, restores our hope, and renews us in new events and relationships.

Question: "Just refuse to do second marriages?"

Wouldn't the 'safest' course be for a minister simply to explain that he has a policy not to do weddings for divorcees? Wouldn't that be simpler and easier?

By what right does a minister of the gospel refuse to officiate a wedding for divorced persons? Far from being a 'safe' course, it seems to me that it is a judgmental action. It communicates that the man or woman in question is somehow permanently flawed or inferior. It reduces him or her to second-class status in the church. But I am not convinced that our Heavenly Father has step-children to be treated differently from his sons and daughters who have the full right to all his blessings and inheritance.

In fairness, I grant that people with this no-second-marriage policy are attempting to be consistent with their understanding of what Holy Scripture says about divorce. One of the reasons for rejecting the rigid view I once held on the subject myself is that it seemed to force me to a posture that looked far more pharisaical than Christ-like in dealing with people. I could perform the wedding of a man or woman who had lived with one or more lovers, had children by one or more of them, and disrespected marriage by refusing to seek legal status for those relationships—and feel good about it. But I could not perform the ceremony of a conscientious person who married too young, tried to make an ill-advised marriage work, but wound up getting a divorce and was now wanting to marry a godly mate—without dishonoring God?

The questions that arise about divorce and remarriage are practically infinite. Every situation is different, with its own special feature that distinguishes it from all others. So I see no point in trying to recall or frame a longer list. I have tried to deal with a broad spectrum of questions in the hope that it is suggestive to the one you would like to ask.

Again, though, hear my disclaimer. And please know that it is offered with sincere humility. *I do not presume to be able to answer all the questions about so complex a matter.* But I am convinced that the pain, failure, and frustration surrounding the topic of divorce must be addressed redemptively. The message of the gospel to every human frustration is grace, pardon, and healing. We must not fail to apply it to the most fundamental of all human relationships.

Do we really think that the sinner whose offense is adultery has no spiritual option in Christ Jesus but to live with his or her brokenness forever? Jesus can heal blind eyes, forgive his own murderers, let drug traffickers and career prostitutes have a full range of life options open to them following conversion but cannot (or will not) heal the broken life of the person who divorces his wife? Worse still, he gives no option to a woman who was divorced against her will if the wretched fellow who tosses her out was not already sleeping with somebody else? Jesus did not put such an impossible burden on human beings. Misguided theologians and teachers did it in his name.

What is Jesus' word to anyone who has been guilty of adultery by virtue of divorce? It is the same word he gave to a woman who had been caught in the very act of adultery and whose life was in jeopardy from some religious people who said they were willing to stone her: "Go your way, and from now on do not sin again" (John 8:11).

We cannot pretend that past failures don't linger in terms of personal pain and consequences to innocent children. Neither can we assume that one's spiritual life does not suffer from the sadness and consternation that most people take away from a divorce. But we can be grateful for God's forgiveness and the chance to begin anew.

A Letter to Divorced Persons

If you have gone through the agony of divorce, my prayer is that this book will be helpful to you.

First, I hope it gives you good information. I am not a psychologist or counselor, and this book is not about methods of coping and getting through the trauma of divorce. I am a Christian theologian. More to the point for this book, however, I am a minister of the gospel. I have been in church ministry for four decades and spent 27 years with the same congregation. Yes, I have been through scores of traumatic situations with people whose life situations are incredibly diverse. No, I didn't know what to do in any of them. Pray, listen, encourage, point to God as loving Father—that was my "strategy" for ministering to persons facing divorce.

Whenever possible, I have helped people find help to address problems, stay together, and reconcile their relationships. When that was not possible, I have typically said, "You do not have to be married to that person any longer, but you must have a relationship with God through Jesus Christ. Don't confuse the two!"

The good information I want you to get from this book has to do with maintaining your relationship with God. Divorce does not have to be the end of your spiritual life. As bad as you feel about what has happened, those "feelings" are not a true index to God's attitude toward you. You have suffered a tragic and painful dissolution of a relationship. Whether your fault, your mate's fault, the fault of both, or "nobody's fault," God deals with you where you are today. He forgives failure. He heals wounds. He helps you move ahead with your life.

Someone's view of divorce and remarriage may have told you otherwise. A few insist that divorced people can't get married again, regardless of the reason for their divorce. More say that divorced people can get married only if they are the innocent parties to a marriage where somebody has been sexually unfaithful; otherwise, for a divorced person to marry is for him or her to be living in adultery. This view means that such a person must either find a way to put the marriage back together or remain single and celibate until death. Those views are mistaken. Some very good people hold them in all good conscience, and you may have been taught some of these things in your church. I was. And I did.

I am convinced by years of study, prayer, and experience that those views are incorrect. In this book, I want to give you good information that will help you read what Scripture says on divorce and remarriage with understanding and confidence. I have tried to write in non-technical language. This is not a book whose goal is to impress "the scholars"; it is intended to give reliable information that is supported by good scholarship to "average church members" who want to understand what the Bible says on this complex topic.

Second, I want to give you confidence about God's grace. All of us must face our past. We must take responsibility for poor decisions and bad behaviors. Christ calls us to repent—that is, change both our minds and our actions—of those decisions and behaviors. Then he asks us to believe that we are forgiven and to let him empower us to move ahead with life under his reign.

Most of us can find it within ourselves to repent of the things we have done that brought pain into our lives—and the lives of others we love. That comes quickly and easily for conscientious souls. What we often have difficulty with is faith. In fact, the more conscientious one is, the harder it usually is for him or her really to believe that God has forgiven some terrible thing. "Yes," she says, "I know the Bible says God puts our sins as far away from us as East is from West, but . . ." But what? He *can't* do that in your case? Or he *won't* do that in your case?

Some of the most conscientious Christians I know come down on themselves harder than anyone else. They tell you quickly how "stupid" the action was and how "terrible" they were to do this or that. All sin is stupid and terrible, but no sin is too great for God to handle. He has taken the initiative through Jesus Christ to provide redemption to thieves and liars, unchaste homosexuals and unchaste heterosexuals, drug traffickers and child molesters, people who have sinned by going through with unjustified divorces and people who are unfeeling and judgmental toward those who have gotten those divorces.

God is in the forgiveness business. And divorce, for all the bad things you may choose to say about it and in spite of all you may have contributed to bringing one about, is not the unpardonable sin. Any sin you confess can be covered by Christ's blood. That includes divorce and remarriage.

Third, I want you to have confidence to move forward with your life. On the view of some, God will forgive a past marital failure. But his forgiveness presumes forfeiting the things most of us want to experience in life—marriage, companionship, sexual intimacy, children/grandchildren, warm family holiday times, etc. Some people sincerely believe that a consequence of divorce is the forfeiture of the right to marry someone else, fulfill the dreams just mentioned, and live within loving family relationships.

In spite of your past, God offers you a future. It is not a partial future. It is not a future shackled to your past. It is a future with the potential for every good thing he has ever dreamed for you. His forgiveness is complete and not partial, absolute and not contingent on your future penance of forfeiting natural human companionship.

May God bless you to read this book with understanding, to receive the fullness of God's grace for your pain (whether self- or other-inflicted), and to rejoice in moving forward as God's pardoned and blessed child.

Rubel Shelly

A Letter to Church Leaders

If you are an elder or deacon, preacher or Bible teacher, you know the subject of divorce and remarriage can be avoided only so long. If you teach through the biblical text, you encounter King David's debacle or try to figure out Hosea's tragic life with Gomer. You are expected to explain Deuteronomy 24 or Matthew 19. Someone asks you a question that is only a slight variant of one you read earlier in this book and recognized. More seriously and painfully, however, you know the subject can't be avoided in terms of the tears, anger, and confusion its terrible reality brings into the lives of people you know and for whose souls you bear a degree of responsibility.

So you read, pray, and study. You walk with fear and trembling into homes where you hope to help save a marriage—and, minimally, to do nothing that would hasten its demise. In spite of all you know to do, however, you will have to watch some people you know and love go through the legal dissolution of their marriages. You will see the impact on their spiritual lives. You will witness the confusion in the lives of their children.

You want to help. But you respect the Word of God and know you must operate within the bounds of its authority. So you try to discover how Scripture can be "useful for teaching, for reproof, for correction, and for training in righteousness" around this complex issue.

This book was written to try to help you understand and teach what the Bible actually says about divorce and remarriage, innocent and guilty parties to marital dissolution, and redemption and healing for divorced persons. As you will discover early on in reading this book, my conviction is that some church leaders have taken a limited number of biblical texts and formulated a punitive theology toward divorce. Those restrictive interpretations and harsh penalties for their violation seem not to have saved very many marriages. Research says that as many marriages end in divorce in conservative Christian churches as in liberal ones or even among unchurched people—perhaps a slightly higher percentage, in fact. Some of Jesus' contemporaries had taken the law about sabbath-keeping that was designed to bless families with time for worship, relaxation, and shared joy over Israel's God and turned it into a rigid set of nearly impossible expectations. They were using a rule meant to protect them to hurt one another. I fear we have done the same thing with some biblical statements about marriage. A rule meant to protect marriage has become a harsh framework for punishing those who fail at it. We have made laws given to bless us into penalties that compel the very people who need God's presence most to flee from him.

The Old Testament holds forth an ideal for marriage but acknowledges the reality of divorce. In a harsh cultural context that took advantage of females generally, Moses was guided to give a law that protected divorced women. It explicitly gave them the right of remarriage and protected them from future interference in their lives by former mates. We have not always seen that law for what it is. We have certainly tended to overlook the context and motivation for it. Divorce was never Plan A for Yahweh's Chosen People, but there was a Plan B for those whose lives were disrupted by it. One so great as King David became a Plan-B man after an affair with the woman who soon thereafter became his wife. He and Bathsheba moved on to build a life together. They did not live in adultery but were truly and legitimately married. Solomon was not their illegitimate child but their son and the heir to Israel's throne—chosen, in fact, over the son of David's first wife. Thus Absalom was rejected in favor of Solomon, as Nathan the prophet made known to all parties involved. Sin and failure led to national turmoil, but Yahweh showed mercy and healed the man after his own heart.

On the view of some, the New Testament has only the Plan-A option for all the Davids and Bathshebas of the world. Make your marriage a success. If you ever divorce, you must be able to prove that you divorced someone who was sexually unfaithful to you—establishing that you are the "innocent party" in such a case. For, it would seem to many, the gospel is more severe with those who fail to keep their marriage vows than was the Law of Moses. But how could that be? There is grace under the Law but inflexibility under grace? Indeed, that paradox seems to be the fact of the matter—if Jesus' rhetorical use of hyperbole is not recognized for what it is and if Paul's teaching given by the Spirit of God is ignored.

So I ask that you read this book as a careful student. Read it as well with a view toward dealing graciously and redemptively with those whose lives are in disarray. Do not retreat from the call for everyone in your church family to embrace God's Plan A: *If you marry, keep your covenant promises with all love and fidelity*. When someone struggles, hold him accountable to his commitments. Pray for her. Offer them professional resources. Do everything within your power to help people live the will of God. Know also that there is a Plan B to God's will that you are authorized to proclaim in every case: *If you fail at your covenant commitment, God is ready to act redemptively in your life*. Some tottering relationships can be pulled back from the brink; some will be too far gone for immediate rescue. Counsel patience. Urge all parties involved to move cautiously and deliberately. Pray for time to reveal options, cool tempers, and dispel fear. Reconciliation may yet be an option. If not, plead with people who are giving up on one another not to give up on God—or to think he has given up on them. Urge repentance for sin. Support counseling and insight for the sake of learning from the past. Focus on mature and holy prospects for the future. And do not fail to hear and repeat Paul's words to those who remarry—even if, in your judgment, too soon or "on the rebound" or to a less-than-ideal partner. "If you marry," wrote the apostle, "you do not sin." Be very cautious that neither you nor those you allow to instruct your church family remove the "not" from the apostle's statement!

Because God is in the forgiveness business, the church must partner with him both to herald and to model redemption in the lives of human beings. That this book could be of help to you in doing just that is my fondest hope and most fervent prayer.

Rubel Shelly

Endnotes

[1]Israel Abrahams, *Studies in Pharisaism and the Gospels, vol. 1* (Cambridge: University Press, 1917), p. 73. Abrahams claims the death penalty for adultery "can never have been frequently enforced....It is not probable that the death penalty for adultery was inflicted at all in the age of Jesus." After describing the procedure of Jewish trials in capital cases generally, Moore observes: "It is clear that with such a procedure conviction in capital cases was next to impossible, and that this was the intention of the framers of the rules is equally plain." George Foot Moore, *Judaism in the First Centuries of the Christian Era, vol. 2* (Cambridge: Harvard University Press, 1927; reprint ed., New York: Schocken Books, 1958), pp. 122-123. Cf. The confrontation between Jesus and certain contemporaries who insisted on stoning a woman "caught in the very act of adultery" at John 7:53-8:11. Jesus was able to show the woman mercy by virtue of the fact that her accusers were not "without sin" in the specific matter at hand. Since a woman had to be found *in coitu* and not simply in a compromising situation, there would have been a notable-by-his-absence male life at stake as well! J. Duncan M. Derrett, "Law in the New Testament: The Story of the Woman Taken in Adultery," *New Testament Studies* 10: 4-5.

[2]David Instone-Brewer, *Divorce and Remarriage in the Bible: The Social and Literary Context* (Grand Rapids: Eerdmans, 2002), p. 23.

[3]Instone-Brewer, *Divorce and Remarriage*, pp. 5-6; "If the owner refuses to provide the female slave with these fundamental rights, he waives his claim of possession, and she is free to go her own way. The provisions here stipulated for such a woman make it very likely that she was not sold into slavery for general purposes, but only as a bride, and therefore with provisions restricting her owner-husband concerning her welfare if he should become dissatisfied with the union. Mendelsohn has cited Nuzian sale contracts which almost exactly parallel the Exodus provisions." John I. Durham, *Exodus* (Waco: Word, 1987), p. 322.

[4]One might think, for example, of the speech of Moses to Israel before his death. The renewal of the berith with Yahweh sounds like what we call a contract: "If you will only obey the Lord your God...but if you will not obey the Lord your God...." (Deut 28:1,15). The conditional terms of blessing were laid out, along with the benefits that would come from the nation's obedience, but so were the curses that would overtake Israel in case of its failure to comply. The irrevocable *berith* that focuses on Messiah and his redemptive mission was, however, very different from the contingency contract about Israel's continued possession of the land promised to Abraham. The promise of

God to be faithful in bringing his great salvific work to completion regardless of Israel's faithfulness or disobedience is called a "new (kind of) *berith*" at Jeremiah 31:31-34. This sense of covenantal faithfulness regardless of the behavior of the other party clearly was not part of the Old Testament notion of *berith* as it relates to marital agreements.

[5]Instone-Brewer, *Divorce and Remarriage*, p. 9. The basis for such an interpretation would have been the common rabbinic principle of interpretation . This tenet is essentially one of logical entailment: If x is true, then y surely follows. In this case the argument would run as follows: If a slave wife has these rights, then surely a free wife would also have equivalent rights. Ibid., pp. 100-101.

[6]Joe M. Sprinkle, "Old Testament Perspectives on Divorce and Remarriage," *Journal of the Evangelical Theological Society* 40/4 (Dec 1977): 535-536.

[7]In the Old Testament literature, one finds the confusing overlap of a faithful presentation of the oppressed situation of females in the Ancient Near East with occasional glimpses of protection for and spiritual service by women that were more in line with the original condition envisioned in Eden and foreshadowed for the church. Thus, on the one hand, there are stories of sexual abuse, polygamy, economic exploitation, and the like. Yet children were taught to honor their mothers as well as their fathers (Ex 20:12; cf. Lev 19:3). There are legal interventions to protect women from certain types of sexual abuse (Ex 21:10-11; 22:16-17). Women could consecrate themselves to the Lord by the Nazirite vow (Num 6:2) and could bring sacrifices and offerings to the Temple. In the absence of male heirs, daughters could receive a family's inheritance and be landowners (Num 27:1ff). And the woman of Proverbs 31 is respected, valued, and praised on her own merits, as well as for her contribution to her husband's standing in the community. Then there are those outstanding women who figure prominently in the Old Testament narrative. They honor God, receive the Spirit of the Lord for ministry, and function on behalf of the larger community. Deborah is included in the list of judges and was a true prophet of Yahweh (Judg 4:4ff). Miriam, the sister of Moses and Aaron, helped them with the leadership of Israel (Ex 15:20-21). There were female Temple singers (Neh 7:67b) and musicians (1 Chron 25:5-6)—as well as "the women who served at the entrance to the tent of meeting" (Ex 38:8).

[8]Instone-Brewer, *Divorce and Remarriage*, pp. 30-31.

[9]Joachim Jeremias, *Jerusalem in the Time of Jesus*, trans. F.H. and C.H. Cave (Philadelphia: Fortress Press, 1969), pp. 308-309; S. Safrai and M. Stern, eds., *The Jewish People in the First Century, vol. 1* (Philadelphia: Fortress Press, 1974), pp. 517-518.

[10]David J.A. Clines, *New Century Bible Commentary: Ezra, Nehemiah, Esther* (Grand Rapids: Eerdmans, 1984), pp. 116-118.

[11]Sprinkle, "Old Testament Perspectives," p. 539. This article raises problems about the translation of 2:14-16 that are ignored here. I am not a Hebrew scholar, cannot comment on proposed emendations of the text or alternative renderings, and have chosen to deal with the statement as it stands and as it is commonly used.

[12]Carlotta Gall, "In Afghanistan, agony as escape: Women fleeing cruel lives choose even crueler deaths," *International Herald Tribune* (March 9, 2004), pp. 1,6.

[13]Robert A. Guelich, *The Sermon on the Mount: A Foundation for Understanding* (Waco: Word, 1982), p. 159.

[14]Dallas Willard, *The Divine Conspiracy* (San Francisco: Harper, 1998), pp. 154-155.

[15]Glen H. Stassen and David P. Gushee, *Kingdom Ethics: Following Jesus in Contemporary Context* (Downers Grove, IL: InterVarsity, 2003), pp. 272-273.

[16]Armand M. Nicholi Jr., *The Question of God: C.S. Lewis and Sigmund Freud Debate God, Love, Sex, and the Meaning of Life* (New York: Free Press, 2002), p. 157.

[17]Guelich, *Sermon on the Mount*, p. 242.

[18]For a scholarly summary of the issues in the Hillelite-Shammaite debate, see Instone-Brewer, *Divorce and Remarriage in the Bible*, pp. 110-117, 133-146.

[19]The rabbinic literature and historical information available to us confirms that divorce was always and only a male initiative in Judaism. Although rabbis eventually agreed that a woman could sue for divorce under certain extreme circumstances, even then the court would require her husband to be the one who issued the certificate of divorce. This unfair situation that made male abuse of women common may lie behind the use of passive verb *moicheuthenai* (to be adulterated) of the divorced woman of Matthew 5:32. This form of the verb may be deliberate for the sake of underscoring the injustice of a woman either being stigmatized as an adulteress by onlookers or being forced against her own will in the matter to be guilty of the (hyperbolic) adultery Jesus assigns to anyone who winds up in a marriage other than his or her original covenant relationship.

[20]The expression literally means "nakedness of a thing" [cf. Francis Brown, S.R. Driver, and Charles A. Briggs, eds., *A Hebrew and English Lexicon of the Old Testament* (Oxford: Clarendon, 1907), pp. 788-789] and, while likely indicating something serious, does not seem to be equivalent to sexual infidelity. It was the term's ambiguity that permitted the rabbinic debates.

[21]Instone-Brewer, *Divorce and Remarriage in the Bible*, pp. 111-112.

[22]The term "guilty party" is typically used of a married person who most directly brings about a divorce by breaking the marriage vows and having an affair; the "innocent party" is thus defined as the person who has made a good-faith effort on behalf of the marriage's success, only to be betrayed by a philandering spouse. In the case of a marriage that ends without third-party involvement, I presume both the husband and wife would be "guilty parties" with equal blameworthiness for the unjustified dissolution of a marriage. As will be explained later, I am not sure this terminology is helpful or meaningful for this discussion. To say the least, the terms do not come from Scripture.

[23]Paul's comment "I wish that all were as I myself am" may be his one concession to those at Corinth who were counseling celibacy as the higher spiritual calling. To forego marriage for the sake of missionary work or some other kingdom endeavor may be a practical and godly decision; to require that people not marry because it puts them closer to God is simply wrong and potentially subjects one to special temptation. Cf. the words of Jesus at Matthew 19:11.

[24]The word "unmarried" in the English text of 8b (NRSV) is supplied by translators and is not another occurrence of the term in the Greek text. *Agamos* occurs a total of four times in the original text of the New Testament, and all of those occurrences are in 1 Corinthians 7.

[25]*New International Dictionary of New Testament Theology, Vol. 3* (Grand Rapids: Zondervan, 1978), s.v. "separate," pp. 536-537.

[26]The apostle's encouragement that anyone among "the unmarried and the widows" should ideally remain "as I am" raises interesting possibilities about Paul's own life situation. Some scholars opine that Paul was married but that, when he accepted Jesus as the Messiah, his wife deserted him. Others speculate that he may have been a widower. Cf. C.K. Barrett, *A Commentary on the First Epistle to the Corinthians* (New York: Harper & Row, 1968), p.161. The answer to these intriguing possibilities is uncertain. Whether Paul had never married, was a widower, or had been divorced does not affect the argument of this chapter.

[27]Although modern jurisprudence has a variety of legal options for dealing with distressed marriages, we must be cautious about reading those back into the biblical text. For example, "separation" as a modern legal term may signify an estrangement of marriage partners wherein each has certain legal protections; a reconciliation effected during a separation does not require formal remarriage by the partners. On the other hand, "divorce" as a modern legal term denotes the dissolution of all legal ties between the parties; a reconciliation brought about after formal divorce would require a new marriage license and a second ceremony for the couple involved. No such distinction existed in the first-century world, whether among Jews or Gentiles. Corinth was a Roman city, and divorce required even less formal steps than Jewish protocol required. Thus an interpreter of 1 Corinthians must understand that "separate," "put away," "divorce," or other equivalent terms used in our English translations signify the same thing—formal dissolution of the marriage bond.

[28]Our canonical Gospels had not been produced at the time of Paul's writing to the church at Corinth. But the words of Jesus from his sermons and dialogues were in widespread oral circulation long before they were committed to writing.

[29]The term *agamos* does not appear in v.27. It seems quite clear, however, that the term *agamos* (used at v.11 of the person who has been divorced) is defined in terms of

what is described here (i.e., someone loosed [a middle/passive form of the verb *luo*] from a bond).

[30]If someone feels that Paul has been slighted here by my failure to include Romans 7:1-3 and 1 Timothy 3, those texts are dealt with in the chapter to follow.

SELECTED BIBLIOGRAPHY

The abbreviated bibliography offered here does not reflect the works consulted or cited in the text of this book. No textual commentaries are listed, for there are simply too many helpful works to begin cataloging them. Journal articles are omitted, for they are accessible through various electronic databases. This short index of recent books is provided for those who wish to study the subject of divorce and remarriage further. Some of the books reflect a point of view compatible with the one presented in this book. For balance and fairness, others reflect positions that disagree with it. The books are listed alphabetically and not in terms of any judgment of importance or value to readers.

Carter, Les. *Grace and Divorce: God's Healing Gift to Those Whose Marriages Fall Short.* San Francisco: Jossey-Bass, 2005.
This book was written by a psychotherapist at the Minirth Clinic and will be of interest principally to Christian counselors, ministers, and other church leaders who are attempting to help people through the personal trauma of marital failure.

Cornes, Andrew. *Divorce & Remarriage: Biblical Principles & Pastoral Practice.* Grand Rapids, MI: Eerdmans, 1993.
This book comes from an Englishman whose goal is to offer "sensitive pastoral application" of the biblical materials for church leaders. It ranges over topics of singleness, marital problems, divorce, reconciliation, and care for divorcees and members of their families.

Instone-Brewer, David. *Divorce and Remarriage in the Bible: The Social and Literary Context.* Grand Rapids, MI: Eerdmans, 2002.
This is a significant scholarly work that examines the biblical texts on divorce and remarriage in light of the first-century Jewish and Greco-Roman world. There is nothing else available with the depth of research reflected in this volume. It is not light reading, but it is rewarding for those who choose to invest the effort.

Instone-Brewer, David. *Divorce and Remarriage in the Church: Biblical Solutions for Pastoral Realities.* Waynesboro, GA: Paternoster, 2003.
A lighter version of the scholarly tome listed above. It offers a summary of the

material in the larger book, stresses issues of pastoral application, and considers questions of the sort that arise in personal and church dilemmas over the subject.

Keener, Craig S. ...*And Marries Another: Divorce and Remarriage in the Teaching of the New Testament.* Peabody, MA: Hendrickson, 1991.
With almost half of this book consumed by endnotes and bibliography, it is more likely to be read by those with some degree of formal biblical training. It is more likely to be helpful with the Pauline materials than in unpacking the Gospels.

Stassen, Glen H. and Gushee, David P. *Kingdom Ethics: Following Jesus in Contemporary Context.* Downers Grove, IL: InterVarsity, 2003.
This thick and sometimes wordy study of the Sermon on the Mount is helpful in setting the words of Jesus on divorce and remarriage in context. The authors' thesis of "transforming initiatives" behind Jesus' interpretation of the Law of Moses is particularly helpful.

Wenham, Gordon J.; Heth, William A.; Keener, Craig S.; and Strauss, Mark L., general editor. *Remarriage after Divorce in Today's Church: 3 Views.* Grand Rapids, MI: Zondervan, 2006.
This book has three writers presenting their own views and responding to those of fellow essayists. One argues that remarriage is never legitimate following divorce; one makes a case for remarriage only in cases of adultery or desertion; and one defends divorce and remarriage under a wider range of circumstances.

Divorce Recovery Resources

"Radical Recovery is a resource guide to help you survive those first awful days, weeks, months, and, of course, all the nights of a mid-life divorce. But the goal is not just survival, it's life-transformation. In spite of your divorce, there is a destiny for you beyond your wildest dreams. Believe that truth and get your new life started today."

THE AUTHOR

"Radical Recovery will shake you out of your lethargy, knock you out of your bitterness, and bounce you out of your self-pity parties. If you want something that is pie-in-the-sky and full of pleasant theories, skip this book. If you want to get better, you have come to the right text."

DAN KNIGHT, OVERLAND PARK CHURCH OF CHRIST, OVERLAND PARK, KANSAS

Radical Recovery
Transforming the Despair of Your Divorce into an Unexpected Good
224 pages $15.99
ISBN 978-0-89112-518-1

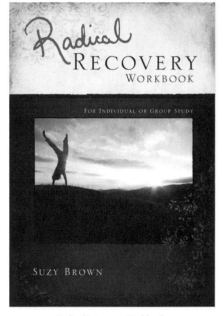

Radical Recovery Workbook
64 pages $9.99
ISBN 978-0-89112-508-2

www.leafwoodpublishers.com

1·877·816·4455

SUZY BROWN conducts divorce recovery workshops and hosts a website: www.midlifedivorcerecovery.com.

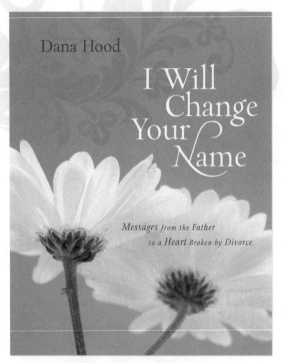